JUANITA BYNUM

Morning Glory

Devotional

Pneuma Life PUBLISHING

Morning Glory Devotional

Unless otherwise noted, Scripture quotations are taken from the King James Version of the Bible.

Scripture quotations noted NIV are taken from the New International Version.
Copyright © 1973, 1978, 1894, International Bible Society.

Copyright © 2000 by Juanita Bynum
Printed in the United States of America
ISBN: 1-56229-150-5

Pneuma Life Publishing
4451 Parliament Place
Lanham, MD 20706
301-577-4052
301-577-4935 (fax)
www.pneumalife.com

TABLE OF CONTENTS

INTRODUCTION

The Bible says that to every thing there is a season, and a time to every purpose under the heaven. Well, my friend, now is the season and this is the time for your purpose in the Lord. I want you to know beyond a shadow of a doubt that this *Morning Glory Devotional* will more than challenge you in some areas; it will change your very life.

In order for it to be most effective, it's going to take more than you reading one or two devotions at your leisure. It's going to cost you more than the price of this book. In order to get you to your next level in God, it's going to take you consecrating yourself and your time unto the Lord as never before. Give up those precious moments in the morning, and gain a priceless relationship with the Lord.

In the morning–before the cares of this life seep in to choke the Word of God from you–devote yourself whole-heartedly unto the Lord. I know that it will be a difficult thing for most to wake up earlier than usual, but press on anyhow . . . give the first fruits of your mind unto He Who suffered and died to save you. Honor, praise, worship and adore the

Lord without the distractions of the world robbing Him of your undivided attention.

Cause me to hear thy lovingkindness in the morning; for in thee do I trust: cause me to know the way wherein I should walk; for I lift up my soul unto thee. Psalm 143:8

In the morning, the Lord will speak to your heart and show forth His loving kindness; will you listen to Him? In the morning, your Savior will be your help, strong tower, refuge, and strength; will you trust in Him? In the morning, He'll show you the way, clear out the path, and order your steps; will you walk therein? In the morning, the Lord will anoint and appoint you, and call you His own; will you lift up your soul to Him?

My brothers and sisters, I do hope that you will rise to this challenge and devote yourselves to seeking the Lord in the morning. Many of these devotions will speak directly into your life, for they were handpicked just for you. The Lord will show forth His glory to you. Seek Him early . . . commune in the *Morning Glory.*

Morning Glory

ASSURED

The LORD *hear thee in the day of trouble; the name of the God of Jacob defend thee; Send thee help from the sanctuary, and strengthen thee out of Zion; Remember all thy offerings, and accept thy burnt sacrifice; Selah. Grant thee according to thine own heart, and fulfill all thy counsel. We will rejoice in thy salvation, and in the name of our God we will set up our banners: the LORD fulfill all thy petitions. Now know I that the LORD saveth his anointed; he will hear him from his holy heaven with the saving strength of his right hand. Some trust in chariots, and some in horses: but we will remember the name of the LORD our God. They are brought down and fallen: but we are risen, and stand upright. Save, LORD: let the king hear us when we call. Psalm 20:1-9*

Psalm 20 is for you this morning. You may think that your spirit has been in the basement for so long that this Scripture couldn't possibly be for you; nevertheless, hearken unto the Word of the Lord. Shake yourself out of any negative mode of thinking and get a hold of what the Lord is saying to you today:

Verse 1: "The LORD hear thee in the day of trouble. The name of the God of Jacob defend thee." You don't have to argue or try to defend yourself. The Lord has heard your prayer, and He has heard your plea. He is the God of you, and He will defend you to the end. Every time you think about being saved, start rejoicing, because you know what? Anytime anyone comes against you, the God of Jacob is going to defend you. Hallelujah! That's enough for you to go ahead and rejoice right now!

Verse 2: "Send thee help from," where? "The sanctuary." Don't stop going to church. More than just a Sunday message awaits you; your help and encouragement shall be found therein. Hebrews 10:25 says, "Not forsaking the assembling of ourselves together, as the manner of some is; but exhorting one another: and so much the more, as ye see the day approaching." Your strength is in Zion today.

Verse 3: "Remember all thy offerings, and accept thy burnt offerings; Selah." The Lord is going to remember all of your offerings. Your offerings and sacrifices have not been forgotten, nor have they been in vain. They are a constant reminder before the Lord. Selah–think on that.

Verse 4: "Grant thee according to thine own" what? Your heart and your own counsel.

Some people have become so dependent on calling prayer lines or their prayer partners that they forego opening up their own mouths and going before the Lord for themselves. The Word says that the Lord will fulfill all of your counsel. That means that you've got to do some talking to the Lord. The prayers of others are good, but you've got to go before the Lord for yourself. There are certain issues that the Lord wants to talk directly to you about.

Verse 5: "We will rejoice in thy salvation . . ." Stop being sad, pitiful, and downtrodden. Salvation has been granted to you, therefore, rejoice! Return unto your First Love today. Ask the Lord to restore unto you the joy of your salvation and uphold you with His free spirit.

" . . . and in the name of our God we will set up our banners: the LORD fulfill all thy petitions." Do you understand how awesome that is? The Lord is granting you unusual favor today.

He is going to fulfill your petitions this morning. Make your request known unto the Lord for He is indeed a prayer-answering God. It is the enemy who constantly seeks to sow seeds of doubt and unbelief into your mind. Refuse to allow him to deceive you into believing that this Scripture is for everyone else but you today. Yes it is! The Lord is getting ready to give you your heart's desires and fulfill the things you've talked to Him about. He's getting ready to send you some help. Prove Him at His Word this morning.

Verse 6: "Now . . ." Is that what your Bible says? It says, "Now." Right now . . . this morning, "know I that the Lord saveth his anointed." Have you ever felt the presence of God, particularly when you are praising Him? Do you know what that is? That is the anointing. Whatever comes against you, the Lord is going to save you, because you are His anointed. Get ready to be rescued this morning.

" . . . He will hear him from his holy heaven with the saving strength of his right hand." The ear of the Lord is inclined unto your prayer today; He is listening intently to your every word. What an awesome God we serve! Trust in His strength this morning . . . the saving strength of His right hand.

Receive and believe His Word today.

Verse 7: "Some trust in chariots, and some in horses: but we will remember the name of the LORD our God." The Lord is Omnipotent and Almighty. There is unequivocally no force that can compare to God's matchless strength. We serve the Creator of all things, and He Who, among countless things, parted the Red Sea. Our God is the same yesterday, today, and forever. That means that you don't have to search the annals of time to find a miracle of God—just take a quick look in the mirror. Some of you have been delivered from some things that no man could have delivered you from. You may have tried every other way before you finally tried God, but He never failed to come through for you. Remember Him this morning. His saving power is available to you today. Conventional methods won't cut it, but the Lord's strength will. He's bringing you out of some things even now as you're reading this.

Verse 8: "They are brought down and fallen: but we are risen, and stand upright." Some situations in your life must fall today—right now—and bow down to the power of God. You may have felt sad, low, depressed, and distressed, but the Lord is going to lift you up this morning. You may have felt knocked down, but you were not knocked out. Arise . . . arise . . . and still I say, arise! Stand up, be strong, and keep you head held high, for, today, the Lord your God is nigh.

Verse 9: "Save, LORD: let the king hear us when we call." You've got to open up your mouth and call upon the Lord today. The breakthrough you need is not going to just jump up off of this page. If you want it, then call Him up!

It doesn't matter if you don't feel like your change is coming. Read Psalm 20 again. It is for you. Write it down. Keep it with you. Put it on your refrigerator if you have to — just don't let it slip away from you. Think about it: What problem, issue, or circumstance can possibly withstand the Word of the Lord? If anyone comes against you, the Lord is going to defend you. Anything that you get into, God is going to save you. Anytime you're weak, the Lord God Almighty is going to strengthen you. Anytime you need to be rescued, He is going to send help. God is going to lift and raise you up this morning, for you are His anointed. He saved you and delivered you; rejoice in your salvation today.

Meditate on Psalm 20 today. If you make a mistake, what are you going to do? Recall the Word of the Lord and pray, "Okay, I may be down right now, but, Lord, You promised me in Your Word that You will raise me up. Though the people on my job may be coming against me, You promised to defend me. Lord, You told me to call unto You, so I lift up my prayer to You right now. Here I am, Lord. I bring my heart before You; I put my trust in You; I place my petitions before You. Help me, Lord. I refuse to live in fear and doubt, because my trust is in Your saving strength. I believe Your Word today. In Jesus' name."

And hereby we know that we are of the truth, and shall assure our hearts before him. 1 John 3:19

Be assured this morning as never before that the Lord has indeed given His promises to you. He will never fail you, leave you, nor forsake you. The Lord is your guarantee!

BEYOND YOUR FEELINGS

As we mature and grow in the things of the Lord, we must all reach the level at which we operate beyond our feelings. In order to be fruitful and effective, we need to be governed by the Holy Spirit rather than the ever-changing needs of our emotions. When feeling discouraged, remind yourself that in Christ, you have all things that pertain unto life and godliness; therefore rejoice! You're not rejoicing because you feel depressed, but because you know in Whom you believe. It's a shame when saints miss God because of walking by their feelings, not by faith.

Many times, your feelings and circumstances may tell you that you are poor, but your faith should rise up and declare, "I believe God and His Word. The Lord shall supply all of my needs according to His riches in glory. I shall prosper and be in good health even as my soul prospers. The Lord has given me the power to get wealth; therefore, I release that power to operate and manifest itself in my life." Your feelings may even say that you are sick and will never get any better, but walk by faith and proclaim, "God has already healed me. My healing shall manifest for by His stripes, I am healed. He sent His Word to heal all of my diseases." Don't allow your feelings to boss you around; bring them under total subjection to the infallible Word of the Lord. Have faith in the midst of adversity—not fear.

For God hath not given us the spirit of fear; but of power, and of love, and of a sound mind. 2 Tim. 1:7

Know the facts, not just your feelings. Know what the Word says about your situation. You may not feel anything when you pray sometimes, but don't allow that to discourage you. God is always there. Declare His Word over all of your concerns.

God hears you when you say, "Lord, I just don't feel anything, but I'm going to praise You anyway. It's just me, Lord. Father, in the name of Jesus, I pray that You will strengthen me." That's a good prayer. It's good because the Lord doesn't have to wait for you to get to the point. Too many people get caught up into declaring what they are feeling instead of what the Lord says in His Word. A prayer that could have taken only 5 minutes suddenly turns into 45 minutes all because they have to *feel* it in order to believe that God truly hears them.

Begin to tap into the realm of prayer, even when it's not convenient to pray. When you're too hot or too cold, too weak or too sick, pray and tell the devil, "You're a liar. My flesh will not govern me. My prayer is unto the Lord. My prayer is my connection to the Almighty One. It's not about what my flesh wants; it's about what my spirit is yearning for. In spite of what I'm going through, my spirit still hungers and thirsts after righteousness. I will not allow my feelings to control me. I bring them under total subjection right now in the name of Jesus."

This morning, I challenge you to go beyond your feelings, whether you feel like it or not. Just when you think that you've exhausted yourself before the Lord, I dare you to press into His presence even further. Refuse to be used against yourself today.

But I keep under my body, and bring it into subjection: lest that by any means, when I have preached to others, I myself should be a castaway. 1 Cor. 9:27

Morning Glory

BINDING AND LOOSING

And I will give unto thee the keys of the kingdom of heaven: and whatsoever thou shalt bind on earth shall be bound in heaven: and whatsoever thou shalt loose on earth shall be loosed in heaven.

Matthew 16:19

When you're praying and seeking God, things have got to be done right; therefore, it is vital that we carefully follow the Lord's instructions. Binding and loosing are key Biblical principles and mighty weapons in prayer. Unfortunately, there are a lot of people who are on a binding binge and are just binding up everything, yet neglecting a huge piece of the puzzle—God's instructions.

"I bind up the spirit of poverty." That's good. "I bind the devil that comes into my house bringing confusion." Okay. So you just got poverty bound up, but you still don't have any money. Confusion is gone, but love still isn't flowing in your house.

1. Key Principle: Never bind up something without loosing something in its place.

When you bind spirits, it leaves an open and clean space. Demonic forces will then scurry around to bring any spirit they can to occupy that vacancy. Contrary to popular opinion, hell has not run out of demons; there is no demon-deficit in hell—a whole line of them are just itching to march right in to an unoccupied vessel.

Read this:

> *And they came over unto the other side of the sea, into the country of the Gadarenes. And when he was come out of the ship, immediately there met him out of the tombs a man with an unclean spirit, Who had his dwelling among the tombs; and no man could bind him, no, not with chains: Because that he had been often bound with fetters and chains, and the chains had been plucked asunder by him, and the fetters broken in pieces: neither could any man tame him. And always, night and day, he was in the mountains, and in the tombs, crying, and cutting himself with stones. But when he saw Jesus afar off, he ran and worshiped him, And cried with a loud voice, and said, What have I to do with thee, Jesus, thou Son of the most high God? I adjure thee by God, that thou torment me not. For he said unto him, Come out of the man, thou unclean spirit. Mark 5:1-8*

When Jesus was confronted by the man full of legions, He didn't stand back talking about, "Umm, will you all come out? You know it's not right to have that many of you in there. That's not fair. Don't you have any manners? Wow, look at him. You're really ruining that man's life. Nobody wants to be around him. It's just not nice to have him behaving like a lunatic and cutting himself all up. Can't you guys quiet down a teeny-weeny bit, just long enough for him to take a quick nap? Pretty please?" No . . . Jesus said, "Come out!" He commanded them to leave.

2. Key Principle: Command with authority.
Read on:

And he asked him, What is thy name? And he answered, saying, My name is Legion: for we are many. And he besought him much that he would not send them away out of the country. Now there was there nigh unto the mountains a great herd of swine feeding. And all the devils besought him, saying, Send us into the swine, that we may enter into them. And forthwith Jesus gave them leave. And the unclean spirits went out, and entered into the swine: and the herd ran violently down a steep place into the sea, (they were about two thousand;) and were choked in the sea. Mark 5:9-13

Not only did Jesus command them to leave, but He also told them where to go!

3. Key Principle: When you bind up a demon and cast it out, tell it where to go.

"Satan come out." Okay, so he's out. He jumped out by virtue of your command and authority, but he still stayed right there in the room waiting for the next opportunity to come back in. Don't you know that if your voice is powerful enough to pull him out, it's also powerful enough to send him somewhere? He must go wherever you command him to go. "You foul and unclean spirit, come out in the name of Jesus. I command you to be cast into the pit, and I send you back to hell where you came from." Now, that's more like it. Don't let the enemy linger around your living room, neighborhood, or anywhere else near your presence. Send him home (hell) where he belongs.

For verily I say unto you, That whosoever shall say unto this mountain, Be thou removed, and be thou cast into the sea; and shall not doubt in his heart, but shall believe that those things which he saith shall come to pass; he shall have whatsoever he saith. Mark 11:23

The mountain was removed, and then what? It was cast into the sea. It had to go somewhere.

Now, I would be remiss to not share a few other things with you. This next nugget of information is going to hurt some feelings, but I have to tell it anyhow: There are some things that you may be binding up that are not about to go anywhere. You could have a binding marathon from dusk 'til dawn, but it still would not make a bit of difference.

"Satan I bind this . . . I bind that . . . "

No, no, no. That may not be the devil, but God!

But the Spirit of the LORD departed from Saul, and an evil spirit from the LORD troubled him. 1 Samuel 16:14

Just as the Lord dealt with Saul, He will also deal with you. Some things that you're binding up, God sent in order to purge your life. How can you discern the difference? Well, when you bind the devil in the name of Jesus, you ought to be able to recognize some results. If none seem to manifest after a while, then what you ought to be saying is, "Okay, Lord. Let Your will be done."

For example, if you're right in the middle of cooking your little beans and things, and you've run out of seasoning salt and don't have two pennies to buy any, you may be led to

say, "Satan, I bind this spirit of poverty and lack." Now, if someone doesn't come in the next few minutes before your meal turns ice cold and say, "The Lord just told me to come by here and give you some salt," then sit on down with those plain beans and say, "Okay, Father, I thank You. There are some people starving right now who are not even blessed with this much." See, the Lord may want you to learn to be content in all things; He may even be calling you to a fast. That's why it is so important to know the Lord's will. Be teachable. Learn the lessons God wants to teach you.

Now that you know how to use these keys correctly, go to it.

Devotional

BLESS THE LORD

A Psalm of David, when he changed his behavior before Abimelech; who drove him away, and he departed. I will bless the LORD at all times: his praise shall continually be in my mouth. Psalm 34:1

There are times when your praise can set you free. Sometimes, you may be waiting for someone else to lead you into praise and worship, but God is saying, "I want you to bless Me." He wants you to bless Him at all times and to praise Him continually—in good times as well as hard times.

Don't wait until you're in church before you bless the Lord. If you've got to have church all by yourself, then go ahead and do that. In fact, the truth of the matter is that you never leave church, because the church is in you. It's not the building that makes the church; you are the church. If you'd do at home what you do in the building, you'd feel church. Bless the Lord while you're washing dishes the same way you bless Him while in the choir stand, and you'll have church. Bless Him in your car the way you do when you're in prayer, and you'll have church. The church is already in you. Your body is the temple of the Holy Ghost, so believe me, any time you want to have church, you can have it.

When you don't see a way out of your circumstances, bless God anyhow. If the Lord has ever brought you out before,

He'll do it again. Trust Him even when you can't trace Him. The reason you may be hindered from blessing the Lord is because you're looking at your situation instead of looking at Him. Don't you know that God is bigger than any problem you've got?

Be aware of the enemy's tactics. The devil never wants you to praise or magnify the Lord, but bless the Lord anyhow. In the midst of your tears, bless the Lord. In the midst of hardship, bless the Lord. In the midst of depression, bless the Lord. He's worthy! The more you bless Him, the more He'll bless you. The more you lift Him up, the more He'll lift you up. Praise God for everything He's ever done, and all that He's going to do. Praise Him for the things that you don't even know He's already taken care of for you.

Go on and bless the Lord this morning. Bless Him like you need Him. You didn't wake up this morning and pick up this book just to prove that you're an avid reader. You've got to do more than just read. Come on and be a participator, and the Holy Ghost will give you a breakthrough. The breakthrough anointing is available to you today.

Get your goal in mind. Whatever you need, go after it in the Holy Ghost. Don't let the devil stop you from getting to your purpose. God is with you always. Feel His anointing and breakthrough power today. Let Him permeate your mind and spirit. This morning, allow the Lord to consume your heart and remove the burden. Let Him take out depression and oppression. He'll rebuke the devourer for your sake today. All you have to do is bless Him.

The Spirit of the Lord is saying to you today, "If you bless Me, I'll break every yoke. If you bless Me, I'll lift the burden. If you bless Me, I'll deliver your mind. If you bless Me, I'll heal your body. If you bless Me, I'll raise you up. If you bless Me, I'll get you out. If you bless Me, I'll bring you into a new anointing; I'll bring you into a new glory; I'll bring you into a new victory. But, I want you to bless Me."

Make up your mind this morning that you're going to bless the Lord at all times. Now, begin to bless Him like it's your last chance. Open up your mouth this morning and bless ye the Lord!

Bless the LORD, O my soul: and all that is within me, bless his holy name. Bless the LORD, O my soul, and forget not all his benefits: Who forgiveth all thine iniquities; who healeth all thy diseases; Who redeemeth thy life from destruction; who crowneth thee with loving kindness and tender mercies; Who satisfieth thy mouth with good things; so that thy youth is renewed like the eagle's. The LORD executeth righteousness and judgment for all that are oppressed. He made known his ways unto Moses, his acts unto the children of Israel. The LORD is merciful and gracious, slow to anger, and plenteous in mercy. He will not always chide: neither will he keep his anger for ever. He hath not dealt with us after our sins; nor rewarded us according to our iniquities. For as the heaven is high above the earth, so great is his mercy toward them that fear him. As far as the east is from the west, so far hath he removed our transgressions from us. Like as a father pitieth his children, so the LORD pitieth them that fear him. For he knoweth our frame; he remembereth that we are dust. As for man, his days are as grass: as a flower of the field, so he flourisheth. For the wind passeth over it, and it is gone; and the place thereof shall know it no more. But the mercy of the LORD is from everlasting to everlasting upon them that fear him, and his righteousness unto children's children; To such as keep his covenant, and to those that remember his commandments to do them. The LORD hath prepared his throne in the heavens; and his kingdom ruleth over all. Bless the LORD, ye his angels, that excel in strength, that do his commandments, hearkening unto the voice of his word. Bless ye the LORD, all ye his hosts; ye ministers of his, that do his pleasure. Bless the LORD, all his works in all places of his dominion: bless the LORD, O my soul. Psalm 103:1-22

Morning Glory

BUILDING YOUR FAITH

How strong is your faith today? Do you honestly believe in God's ability and that the Lord will do just what He said He would? If you're finding it difficult to trust solely in the Lord, then I'm afraid that you may not know His works. When you read the Word of God, you know that the same God that parted the Red Sea, provided manna for the children of Israel, changed water into wine, and raised the dead is the same God that's in operation in your life this morning. The more you read God's Word and get to know His personality, the more you realize that the Lord can do anything but fail.

Resolve to start increasing your faith today. Believe God as never before to be your Healer. You may want to start out with just a headache. Vow today that every time you get a headache, you won't take an aspirin or pain reliever, but will pray instead and believe God to heal you of that headache. Now perhaps you may still want to take an aspirin for a toothache, but whenever a headache surfaces, you're going to learn how to believe God.

Please do not misunderstand me . . . I am not advocating that you throw away all of your medicines and forever writhe in pain. The point being made is that if you never give God an opportunity to prove Himself, you'll never know what He can do. If you never develop the faith to believe the Lord to heal you of a headache, then if it became necessary for you to believe Him to heal cancer, you may not be able to do so; He's the same God. How are you going to get down on your knees and believe Him to deliver your family if you can't even believe Him for yourself? You need to know that God is Who He says He is. This isn't about testing God; it's about testing your faith.

Develop your spiritual resume. Sometimes, the people of God ought to stop crying and understand they are being taught and trained. Some need to learn how to get through some of their bills until the Lord provides. Once they've overcome that bill and face a similar situation, they then can confidently rebuke the devil; they would have developed their spiritual resume and attained experience in that area.

Determine now to stay in the fire long enough for God to prove Himself. You've got to know for yourself what God can do. You can't just depend on my testimony or your grandmother's testimony. You've got to have your own valley experience with God. When He brings you out, you'll be able to add that to your spiritual resume and tell the devil, "Satan, you're a liar. Last year when I was sick, and the doctor said that I would not get well, the Lord healed my body. I know the Word for myself and have seen it operate in my life. You better back on up, because by His stripes, I am healed!"

It's faith building time this morning. When the storm hits in your life, there won't be any time for you to wonder if God can come through for you—you'll need to know that He can.

Devotional

Don't sway, but stand strong and please the Lord with your faith today.

But without faith it is impossible to please him: for he that cometh to God must believe that he is, and that he is a rewarder of them that diligently seek him. Hebrews 11:6

CANCELING THE LIE

Howbeit when he, the Spirit of truth, is come, he will guide you into all truth: for he shall not speak of himself; but whatsoever he shall hear, that shall he speak: and he will shew you things to come. John 16:13

If the Holy Spirit, Who is the Spirit of truth, leads and guides you into all truth, then that must mean that once truth comes, it cancels every lie of the devil that's ever lived in you. The lie that whispers that you can't make it; the lie that yells you're too weak; the lie that tries to convince you that you're not an overcomer; the lie that taunts you into believing that you're never coming out of your situation; the lie that tells you to quit and give up—all of those lies are canceled, for you've been led into all truth. When you received the Holy Ghost, He led and guided you to the truth that says:

I can do all things through Christ which strengtheneth me. Philip. 4:13

Stop whining and complaining. You've been given a new life, not a new lie. Are you still acting depressed and like you can hardly make it? Then, you need to go back to the altar and tarry until you're baptized and filled with the Holy Ghost. Once you receive it, every lie of the devil is canceled out of your life. It cancels every alcohol devil, every lust spirit, every generational curse, and every lying spirit. You shall not die of cancer, because by His stripes you are healed; the generational curse is broken. You shall not live in poverty, for you've been given the power to get wealth. You are not weak and worthless, for you are more than a conqueror.

Now unto him that is able to do exceeding abundantly above all that we ask or think, according to the power that worketh in us, Ephes. 3:20

You've been living a lie too long. Realize that the power of the Lord is working in you. You are going to make it. You're in a win/win situation in which you cannot lose. Even when you're confused and you don't know what to pray for, guess what?

Likewise the Spirit also helpeth our infirmities: for we know not what we should pray for as we ought: but the Spirit itself maketh intercession for us with groanings which cannot be uttered. And he that searcheth the hearts knoweth what is the mind of the Spirit, because he maketh intercession for the saints according to the will of God. Romans 8:26-27

This day, the lie shall die.

And ye shall know the truth, and the truth shall make you free.
John 8:32

Be made free today. There's truth in God's Word. Speak God's truth and kill the lies over your family, finances, health, relationships, church, and life in Jesus' name. This morning, practice speaking words of life, not the devil's lies.

Devotional

CIRCUMCISING YOUR MIND

During the circumcision process, excess flesh is cut away from the working organ because it is in the way and cannot produce anything. It is a hindrance. In Old Testament times, circumcision was required in order to enter into covenant with the Lord. In order to be declared worthy for the Master's use, one had to be circumcised.

And ye shall circumcise the flesh of your foreskin; and it shall be a token of the covenant betwixt me and you. Genesis 17:11

This morning, God wants to be your spiritual neurosurgeon and cardiologist. When you've got an uncircumcised heart and mind, the fleshly and unsevered part is constantly flapping in the way. That's why you may be hitting and missing in prayer . . . sometimes blessed, then sometimes not.

Although you are a chosen child of the Lord with a destiny and a purpose, if you're still operating with an uncircumcised mind, then some things that you pray for will not come to pass. If you are praying in the will of your flesh, then you are praying amiss and not in the will of God.

For my thoughts are not your thoughts, neither are your ways my ways, saith the LORD. Isaiah 55:8

Morning Glory

Examine your ways and totally surrender yourself to the Lord this morning. Let Him circumcise you under the knife of His Word. Ask Him to cut out every thing that is not of Him. Circumcise your mind. Circumcise your thought life. Circumcise your desires. Circumcise your will. Circumcise your actions. Let the Lord pierce you thoroughly this morning.

For the word of God is quick, and powerful, and sharper than any twoedged sword, piercing even to the dividing asunder of soul and spirit, and of the joints and marrow, and is a discerner of the thoughts and intents of the heart. Hebrews 4:12

Circumcise your heart today that you may live.

And the LORD thy God will circumcise thine heart, and the heart of thy seed, to love the LORD thy God with all thine heart, and with all thy soul, that thou mayest live. Deut. 30:6

CONSISTENCY

Being consistent means that you generally hold to the same principle or practice. For many, the only thing they are consistent with is their changeable and flighty ways.

When inconsistent in your relationship with the Lord, you are not on one accord with Him. Do you know that consistency will march you right to the door of your miracle? Inconsistency will sink it's clutches into you and cause you to stop at the wrong time? It holds on like a grapple hook and will cause you to miss countless blessings.

The soul of the sluggard desireth, and hath nothing: but the soul of the diligent shall be made fat. Proverbs 13:4

Resolve now to finish whatever you started this year. If you're going to workout at the gym, then don't even sign your name on the contract if after one week, you'll miss a day, and then give up altogether. At that rate, how can God trust you to run your own business, and you can't even be consistent enough to take your hips to the gym regularly? If you can't be counted on to attend your current job, then why in the world would the Lord bless you to run a multi-million dollar company? You would barely show up for work! Instead, you would muster up some flimsy excuse like you couldn't go in because you had a little cough. Don't you know that some people are so diligent on their jobs that they would almost have to be taken out on a stretcher before they'd miss a day at work?

Seest thou a man diligent in his business? He shall stand before kings; he shall not stand before mean men. Proverbs 22:29

Have you ever said, "I want to be just like Jesus"? Well, Jesus didn't walk worthy one day, then unworthy the next. He was consistent. If you really want to be Christ-like, then you've got to stop procrastinating and dragging your feet; be consistent in your walk with the Lord.

If you always wanted to be a college graduate, then I don't care if you've got to take one class a semester, be consistent with it. You may not graduate until you're 80 years old, but at least you didn't give up; you brought closure to it. If you started sewing a dress last year and stopped one sleeve short, then go back and finish the sleeve, even if you aren't going to wear the dress.

Many have a major problem with starting things and stopping short of the goal. They may be true visionaries, but they lack the follow-through and perseverance to actually make their dreams a reality. Let's say they started a "Win-the-World in 30 Days" campaign. You can just about guess what happened on the 29th day: "Well, I was going to do it, but they got in my way. They didn't like me, so I didn't finish. See, something happened, and that's the reason why I just couldn't accomplish that thing. What they did was . . ."

All of a sudden, it's everybody else's fault as to why they couldn't complete their goal. One of the first steps towards breaking out of inconsistent behavior is to be accountable and responsible for your own actions, or lack thereof. In order to destroy that inconsistent chief, you have to recognize the power of opposition for what it is. Opposition is supposed to add some substance to what you're doing.

When you are inconsistent, you are content to get stuck and sink into a rut. Instead of using opposition as a tool to strengthen you, it becomes your excuse for weakness; then that's the very excuse you need to procrastinate; then that's the very excuse you need not to succeed; then that's the very excuse as to why you haven't accomplished what you were supposed to accomplish; then you play the name-&-blame game because so-and-so did this-and-that, which is the reason you couldn't do whatever you were supposed to do. Seems like the only thing you're consistent at is being inconsistent.

Remember: Consistency works every time—positively as well as negatively. For example, if you wanted to lose your "love handles", what were you consistent with doing? Eating fast foods, or exercising and changing your diet? Like I said, consistency works every time.

This morning, get a new composition book. Don't use it for anything else. Grocery lists aren't for this notebook. Get something else for your "things to do" list, because this is not for that purpose. Write down all of your inconsistencies in this new notebook. Examine yourself and your habits thoroughly and write down all of the things that you need to change. Then, be consistent about changing those things. Write down realistic timeframes for accomplishing your goals. Search yourself. Be honest with yourself, and, finally, be consistent.

DESTROYING THE YOKE

The power of God is so incredibly awesome and full of purpose. How is it that so many use it as their new drug of choice to only bring about an emotional feel-good? The power of God should be used for what it is supposed to be used for—the anointing.

The anointing is not only a burden lifter, but it also destroys whatever yokes hinder you from becoming all that God purposed for you to be. The difference between you and someone unsaved is that the anointing allows you to live a fulfilled human life. It equips you to break barriers that hinder the average human being. If barriers are not being broken in your life, then I'm sorry to have to be the one to tell you, but you do not have the Holy Ghost, and you are not anointed.

Have you ever seen people just talking in tongues but aren't doing a thing?

"Are you going to go to work today?"

"Oh, the Lord just told me to stay home . . . (tongues)."

Wait, wait, wait. Come up out of those tongues! Your tongues aren't going to keep your lights on. When it's time for the rent to be paid, your landlord isn't going to want to hear your tongue-talking self; he's going to say, "Give me my money, now!"

Whenever you feel the anointing of God, it comes to

change something that you couldn't change yourself. Something was just quickened alive in you, something was just taken out, and something was just put in. If you were depressed and praised God and felt His anointing, then that anointing came to lift the burden and destroy the yoke of depression. We need to get to the point where we can believe God to work something out for us even when there's no organ playing, drum beating, or choir singing in the background. If not, then we will become a bunch of fanatically emotional people. Emotionalisms may entertain, but they cannot change a thing.

When you get saved and filled with the Holy Ghost, the fullness of God enters your life and begins to develop a different appetite within you. Before you personally accepted Jesus, you were among the living dead. The spirit of destruction was in operation in your life, which explains why you were doing things to destroy yourself; you were merely following after the spirit that lived in you. When you became born-again, that spirit of destruction went out, and the Spirit of life everlasting walked in. Now, you yearn for greater things and desire to be used mightily by the Lord. Do you know why? The Holy Spirit is telling you the truth about yourself. He tells you that you are not poor—you're wealthy; you're not sick—you're well; you're not discouraged—you're encouraged; you will not die—you'll live. You're simply following after the new Spirit that is now dwelling within you.

Learn how to experience, walk in, and embrace the

anointing everyday. Communicate with the Holy Spirit. "Okay, which way? Holy Ghost, how do I do this? What should I do when I get over there?" Allow the Holy Spirit to lead and guide you into all truth. Although your spirit is always working, your flesh tries to hinder your spirit from getting you to your next level in God. You'd be surprised at the things you could accomplish if you just stopped obeying the desires of your flesh. Your future is already set; it's already in you. Get your flesh out of the way.

If you want to go to graduate school, then you don't have to get on your knees and pray, "Lord, help me. I really want You to just put it in my spirit. I want to go to school." Look, graduating with a Master's degree is already in you. What you should be praying is, "Holy Ghost, kill my flesh. Let all of this inconsistency and procrastination cease. Destroy this yoke."

According as his divine power hath given unto us all things that pertain unto life and godliness, through the knowledge of him that hath called us to glory and virtue: 2 Peter 1:3

If you are filled with the Holy Ghost, then the power that knows all things and sees all things is already within you. When you have the Holy Ghost, you can walk into a building you'd like to work at, and God will tell you right in your spirit what's available and what's not. "It's a job available in the mail room. Stay right here, and don't say anything. Don't mention the fact that you have a degree because you need a job right now. Don't say anything to that person because he's not the one you need to speak to. Go back tomorrow. Get up now and put on your clothes, because today is the day." That's powerful.

We have the Holy Ghost in order to succeed. He doesn't dwell in you just for your emotions; He's F.Y.I.—for your information. How, then, can we fail when the Spirit is telling us the secrets? How can we not succeed when God has unequivocally given us all things that pertain unto life and godliness? What excuse can there be when the yoke has been utterly destroyed?

I want you to know that the Holy Spirit will destroy the yokes and barriers for you this morning. Will you begin to walk by faith, or will you keep wondering whether or not He's done it? He has equipped you to soar beyond hindrances and limitations, but you've got to decide to stop hiding. Trust the Lord to order your footsteps. Hearken unto His voice this morning. Abide in Him, and He will abide in you. Be confident in Him. He's reminding you today that His yoke is easy and His burden is light, so cast all of your cares on Him. Bask in His anointing this morning. His anointing will destroy the yoke.

Devotional

Morning Glory™

DON'T GO BACK

The Lord wants to remind you this morning that He hand-picked you. Everyone in the world isn't saved because, first of all, not everyone is chosen; yet you are His chosen one. There are a lot of people professing to be Christians who really are not. That's why people that say they're saved but act like the devil shouldn't discourage you. They may have heard the plan of salvation and liked it, but they never received the revelation of salvation; therefore, they cannot live it.

The bottom line is that we cannot keep mistreating God—wanting to be saved today and wishing we weren't tomorrow. It's time to stop flipping back and forth and playing Ping-Pong with your salvation. Too many people get caught up into thinking that because we serve a merciful God, He's some kind of a gullible weakling. Too many think that they can outwit the Lord, use Him up, and go back to Him when it's convenient for them. Understand something: You cannot come unto the Lord unless He calls you; so, you'd better stay yourself put because He may not call you again.

Seek ye the LORD while he may be found, call ye upon him while he is near: Isaiah 55:6

Some of your friends may still be in the bar smoking, drinking, cursing, and sleeping around. Leave them there—

don't get sucked back into that lifestyle. Why do you suppose they're not thinking about being saved? Because they cannot come unto the Father unless He calls them. Yet, God chose you and drew you near to Him; never take that for granted. Pray for their salvation and that the Lord sends people to minister to them, and never fail to be a good witness before them. Intercede for them, but make sure you do not entangle yourself by getting caught up in your old ways, trying to relive your old days.

> *Let the wicked forsake his way, and the unrighteous man his thoughts: and let him return unto the LORD, and he will have mercy upon him; and to our God, for he will abundantly pardon. For my thoughts are not your thoughts, neither are your ways my ways, saith the LORD. For as the heavens are higher than the earth, so are my ways higher than your ways, and my thoughts than your thoughts. Isaiah 55:7-9*

Do you know that you did not just make up your mind one day to be saved? If your mind got made up to be saved, then know that it was the mercy of God that jumped into your mind, turned it around, set your body to church, got you up out of your seat, and brought you to the altar. Somebody that you don't even know interceded for you. Your parents may have prayed for you. You may not have been raised up in the church, didn't know anybody that was sanctified, and surely didn't know anybody full of the Holy Ghost; yet, one glorious day, you fumbled into a church and before you knew it, tears came rolling down your cheeks. Your heart and mind were changed because of the amazing grace of God.

For, by grace are ye saved through faith; and that not of yourselves: it is the gift of God: Not of works, lest any man should boast.

Ephesians 2:8, 9

Jesus suffered, bled, and gave His life for you—what else can He give?

For it is impossible for those who were once enlightened, and have tasted of the heavenly gift, and were made partakers of the Holy Ghost, And have tasted the good word of God, and the powers of the world to come, If they shall fall away, to renew them again unto repentance; seeing they crucify to themselves the Son of God afresh, and put him to an open shame. Hebrews 6:4-6

Don't crucify our Lord all over again. You don't have to backslide. You don't have to go back to your old ways. Don't try to prove that you can relive your old days. Salvation is your blessing, not your burden. The road is straight and narrow and eternal life awaits. Stop looking to the left and to the right—keep your eyes and mind focused on the Lord. You know the warning signs. You've seen your way of escape. You know when you're being tugged back into a life of sin. It's not worth it. Whatever momentary thrill you think you're going to get, I promise you, its not worth kicking God out of your life—even for a second—to do it. Count the cost, my brothers and sisters. Count the cost. Look beyond the moment, for sin is never without its consequences. The wages of sin is still death, and I'll tell you again, nothing is worth that.

Be diligent in your walk with God and do not become weary in your well-doing. The Lord chose you. He wants you to know this morning that He loves and cares about you. He loves you more than anyone in this world. He loves you more than that person that may be urging you to forget Him. Don't do it—don't go back. The Lord trusted you to receive His revelation; don't betray Him. Conquer each day, one day at a time. You can make it. Lean and depend on Him; He'll help you, so hang on in there. Draw nigh unto Him, and let this be your prayer this morning:

Restore unto me the joy of thy salvation; and uphold me with thy free spirit. Psalm 51:12

Devotional

Morning Glory

DRINKING FROM LIVING WATERS

Then cometh he to a city of Samaria, which is called Sychar, near to the parcel of ground that Jacob gave to his son Joseph. Now Jacob's well was there. Jesus therefore, being wearied with his journey, sat thus on the well: and it was about the sixth hour. There cometh a woman of Samaria to draw water: Jesus saith unto her, Give me to drink. (For his disciples were gone away unto the city to buy meat.) Then saith the woman of Samaria unto him, How is it that thou, being a Jew, askest drink of me, which am a woman of Samaria? for the Jews have no dealings with the Samaritans. Jesus answered and said unto her, If thou knewest the gift of God, and who it is that saith to thee, Give me to drink; thou wouldest have asked of him, and he would have given thee living water. The woman saith unto him, Sir, thou hast nothing to draw with, and the well is deep: from whence then hast thou that living water? Art thou greater than our father Jacob, which gave us the well, and drank thereof himself, and his children, and his cattle? Jesus answered and said unto her, Whosoever drinketh of this water shall thirst again: But whosoever drinketh of the water that I shall give him shall never thirst; but the water that I shall give him shall be in him a well of water springing up into everlasting life. John 4:5-14

Have you ever gone before God and said, "Lord, I'm thirsty"? You know that the well of living water inside the Spirit of God is deep, but you just can't seem to find anything to draw it out with. Your cup may be so full of the people, things, and situations you've been involved in, until it seems as if there's no place for the Lord. You may be going back and forth to the same church, yet still finding yourself thirsty Sunday after Sunday. Hungering and thirsting after right-eousness is one thing, but starving in your spirit is something altogether different. It may even seem as if you've reached a desert place in your life where people are sucking you dry. When you feel that way, examine how you're going to the well. The problem may lie in the fact that you've been searching for a drop from outside sources when what you really need to do is tap the well within yourself.

When the Holy Spirit dwells within you, there is so much anointing and power flowing on the inside that every time you have a need and you're thirsty, all you need to do is prime the pump and say, "Spring up, O well." No one is going to prime the pump for you; that responsibility is your own. If you want your well to spring up so that you can drink from living waters and experience the power of God, then you have got to prime your own pump.

This morning, remember a time when the power of God operated in your life. Grab a hold of that thing and begin to thank the Lord for it. Thank Him until you feel your well filling up with water. I'll tell you right now that this isn't an intellectual exercise; it's a spiritual assignment. The Lord is saying that this water isn't just shouting or dancing water. The water in your well is resurrection water. If you can feel the power of God anywhere on you this morning, He's resurrecting something that the devil killed in your life.

Understand something: This prophecy is for you this morning. Of the billions of people in this world, you didn't just pick up this book, turn to this page, and read these words by happenstance. This is for you. I don't care if your mother gave this book to you, your co-worker loaned it to you, or you found it on the local subway, this is for you today.

Your ministry is getting ready to get up. Your family is getting ready to get up. Your finances are getting up. Your praise and worship are getting up. The Lord is telling you today that if you want to live, begin to say "yes". If you want to live, begin to praise Him. If you want to live, begin to shout out of your belly. Out of your belly is going to spring up enough anointing to wash out everything that's not like God.

He that believeth on me, as the Scripture hath said, out of his belly shall flow rivers of living water. John 7:38

God is saying to you, "Live!" In spite of what you're going through, live. No matter what the doctor said, live. It doesn't matter what kind of family you came out of, God said live. The resurrection power lives within you. Don't look at your situation and become discouraged, because where death seems prevalent, so is redemption and the resurrection power of God. Look at your circumstance and say, "It's not going to stay like that—not as long as I'm here—because when I come around, living water springs from me. This thing has got to get up . . . it has got to live again. Spring up, in Jesus' name."

"Satan, the Lord rebukes you. I command you to remove every stop that you've put in the lives of these readers. I command dead relationships to be severed. I command every cancerous thing that is eating up their spirit and anointing to dry up and die. I command you to loose your hold and flee. Holy Ghost, have your way. Spirit of God, I release you into the homes, lives, minds, bodies, and spirits of every person reading this. We thank you for it now, Lord. In Jesus' name. Amen."

New life, new joy, and new hope are springing up within you right now. Receive it. Can you feel your living water? Can you feel it? Come on, hit your belly and sing, "Spring up, O well."

Then Israel sang this song, Spring up, O well; sing ye unto it:

Numbers 21:17

Morning Glory

EMBRACING CHANGE

When something changes, there's no need in becoming undone because change is supposed to happen. In fact, change always occurs for your benefit. There are some comfortable areas in our lives where if change did not come, we'd still be stuck in those things until Jesus returns.

Stop letting change impact you negatively. Learn how to operate in it and use it as a tool for your maturity. Question yourself, "Okay, I'm changing in this. This isn't the way it used to be. What level am I to operate at now? What's going on in my life?"

Sometimes the Lord is urging us to change certain areas in our lives. He'll say, "I want you to learn how to communicate; I want you to learn how to not get so angry and watch your temper." Unfortunately, we often do not heed the lessons of the Lord.

Know this: The Lord will never allow you to stay untaught. If He's trying to teach you a lesson about your emotions, then you'll learn it one way or the other. If He's telling you to watch your tone of voice and how you behave, then certain situations will line up in your life to make sure you correct that facet of your life. For instance, someone may do something that would usually upset you. Rather than succumbing to strife, you'll remind yourself to watch your temper. That is embracing change in your life.

Now, you'll either learn that way, or the Lord will set you up in another situation where you'll have to learn the hard way. You could be in a crowded church hallway just after the service ended, and because someone bumped you the wrong way, you start a yelling match in front of everybody. Because of your rambunctious and disorderly behavior, you're finally forced to change. Your embarrassment provoked you to humility. Perhaps the next time you'll pay a little more attention to God when He's trying to change you for your own good.

Do you know that you will never know what is in you until you're pressed out? Can you stand the pressure? Will you change for the better?

"Well, I never really finished school, and I'm trusting God to bless me with that."

College isn't in your house! You've got to get up and go to school. Nobody is going to knock on your door and say, "Excuse me. Did you want a Master's Degree? I sensed that in my heart when I was at the admission's office. Your name and address just came up in my spirit, and something told me to come and bestow one upon you." Yeah, right!

Just like Gideon, a lot of us need to lighten our load today. Gideon had too many people in his camp, and, therefore, had to forsake quantity in order to have quality. The people around him had to be the right kind of people. Being laden with too many of the wrong people is a sure-fire way to stunt

your spiritual growth in God.

This morning, write down the things that you need to change. Be honest with yourself. If you are quick to have an attitude and fly off of the handle, then you should know that you need to change that area of your life. Search yourself and change.

Know this: From this day forward, you are not going to be pitiful. You are not going to keep crying. You are not going to be a wimp or afraid. You are not going to be cast down or burdened. You're not going to be distressed or depressed, over-whelmed or overtaken. You will not be fearful or frustrated, worn out or weary.

You're going to be saved. You're going to be defended. You're going to be charged with a new strength and a new power. You are God's anointed. In fact, you need to just say that aloud; "I am God's anointed. He protects His anointed; He takes care of His anointed; He brings His anointed out."

This is a different day for you today. This isn't yesterday or yesteryear. You're not even the same person you were then. Come up out of the past. This is a new era in your life. Refuse to be a new person living in an old world. Refuse to be a new person living in an old year. You're new. Whatever you didn't accomplish in the past, forget it. Don't let that hold you back. Have the courage to start all over again. Whatever area you failed in before today, let it go. You are not the same person that failed. You changed.

There's a whole new commission and brand new direction

for your life. Don't let the enemy get you stuck in your old order. Don't get stuck trying to finish the old order of an old year just because you created your own deadline to get that thing completed. If you didn't finish it and you missed your deadline, don't keep banging your head against the walls of procrastination, condemnation, and regret. Change.

How long are you going to keep thinking about what you could have done, should have done, and would have done? How many times are you going to regret not being where you want to be in your life if only you hadn't done such and such? Constant regrets are just causing you to halt positive change from occurring in your life.

Some of you don't understand how deep this is. Sometimes, you've even got to go as far as changing your wardrobe, because you're just not the same person anymore. Some of you are going to have to move out of the neighborhood you're in; you're not the same person anymore. It's a brand new day. This is a new era for you.

The Lord is going to save you, raise you up, give you strength, and send you help. Everything you need is going to be there for you, if you'll only dare to embrace change and change. If you never embrace change, regret will constantly besiege you and make you very miserable. You'll always measure yourself by what you should have done, rather than what you actually had the courage and faith to do.

Embrace change this morning—don't run from it. If you have to read this one devotion everyday until it seeps deep down in your spirit, then do that. Don't be afraid. The Lord has blessed you with everything you need. Your dreams and your goals are from Him. Everything you need, He's already placed within you. Begin to birth change in your life. Push yourself. Set daily goals, and don't allow your past to become your prison. Break out. You can make it. Tell yourself that you can do it. If you never hear a single person affirm your dreams and tell you that you can do this, then just begin to prophesy to yourself.

Change. Push it through. Birth it this morning. Travail and weep for it. Break condemnation and every force that binds you up. You're pushing yourself to a new level. Push it through. You were not given the spirit of fear, but of love, power and a sound mind. Put a demand on God this morning. Let His Word come alive in your spirit.

When you enter into prayer today, tell the Lord that you want to be changed. Ask Him to help you embrace change as never before. Tell the Lord that above anything else, you want His will to be done in your life. I cannot stress that enough. It is His will that is ushering in change this morning. It is so critical at this point in your life that you do not act on your own self-imposed will. Don't get caught outside of God's special grace today by making changes not commissioned by Him. Allow the Lord's kingdom to come and His will to be done in your life.

Call on the anointing to go into the crevices of your mind and the depths of your spirit, and pull out everything that's unlike the Lord.

My friend, you are entering into spiritual warfare this morning to kill your consistent resistance to change. Annihilate your rebellion to making the changes God ordained for your life. Destroy the very root of disobedience in your life. Make sure that you grab a hold of this; God is giving you a special grace to embrace change this morning. He's redirecting your course. He's shifting you to your next level. Be willing to undergo the transformation. Bind up fear, and loose your faith today. Take the opportunity to give God the praise. He is your protection, your leader, your guide, and He is your Spirit of truth. It's time to grow up, mature, and embrace change today, in Jesus' name.

Morning Glory

FASTING

Is it such a fast that I have chosen? a day for a man to afflict his soul? is it to bow down his head as a bulrush, and to spread sackcloth and ashes under him? wilt thou call this a fast, and an acceptable day to the LORD? Is not this the fast that I have chosen? to loose the bands of wickedness, to undo the heavy burdens, and to let the oppressed go free, and that ye break every yoke? Isaiah 58:5-6

"Lord, I just want to be used . . . I want to be so powerful in You that I think I'll go on a 21-day fast."

If that's the reason you fast, then you might as well go eat. You shouldn't fast for power. You fast to kill the flesh so that the power that's already in you can manifest. Don't get caught up into fasting for the wrong reasons. Instead of wasting time laying down your plate thinking that's going to give you more power, take the death walk. The more flesh you put to death, the more God can be resurrected within you. When the resurrection power of God steps in, you don't want it battling against your will.

In order to be purged, fast. You don't have to fast for your anointing because the day that you got saved, everything God was going to use you to be jumped in. Your calling was established the day of your salvation. You were an evangelist at the altar. You became a preacher the day you said, "Father, come into my life and forgive me for all of my sins". Fasting moves your flesh out the way so that the real call of God in you can come forth and manifest in your life. So when you fast, do it to be cleansed, broken, and emptied out. Fast so that every foul spirit that's unlike God will flee.

> *For I know that in me (that is, in my flesh,) dwelleth no good thing: for to will is present with me; but how to perform that which is good I find not. For the good that I would I do not: but the evil which I would not, that I do. Now if I do that I would not, it is no more I that do it, but sin that dwelleth in me. I find then a law, that, when I would do good, evil is present with me. Romans 7:18-21*

The Apostle Paul is saying that there is a constant battle of good and evil being waged within you. When you yield yourself to the Lord by fasting, you cause that battle to cease. Because there is a divine purpose for your life, the Lord is not going to let even you get in the way. He will start processing you and bringing you into the things that He has ordained and predestined for you. If you resist Him, you will find yourself being quite miserable. If you do not willfully submit to His process, then every time you desire peace, the Lord will remind you, "I want My will to be done in you, not your will." There will be a constant warfare on the inside of you until you totally yield unto the Lord.

Fasting is a key to yielding totally unto the Lord. Paralyze your flesh and bring it under subjection to the will of the Lord, and get God's Word into your spirit. If you can only

Devotional

fast for a day, a meal, or a snack, surrender yourself to His will today and receive His reward.

Moreover when ye fast, be not, as the hypocrites, of a sad counte-nance: for they disfigure their faces, that they may appear unto men to fast. Verily I say unto you, They have their reward. But thou, when thou fastest, anoint thine head, and wash thy face; That thou appear not unto men to fast, but unto thy Father which is in secret: and thy Father, which seeth in secret, shall reward thee openly. Matthew 6:16-18

Morning Glory

FROM CARNAL TO SPIRITUAL

Be sober, be vigilant; because your adversary the devil, as a roaring lion, walketh about, seeking whom he may devour: 1 Peter 5:8

Ladies and Gentlemen: We are in the heat of the battle. I promise you, being saved and staying saved is not some simple game. The attacks from the enemy are very real, no matter how subtle they may seem. Satan desires to have you, that he may sift you as wheat. Therefore, be sober and vigilant, because your adversary, the devil, is walking about like a roaring lion seeking to devour you!

For to be carnally minded is death; but to be spiritually minded is life and peace. Romans 8:6

When you live in carnality and not in the Spirit, Satan has a right to walk in and do to you what he wills, when he pleases. Why? Because you are on his territory. He wants to make you his POW—Prisoner of War. You see, instead of being a doer of God's Word, carnality causes you to be MIA—Missing in Action.

When your mind reverts from the spiritual to the carnal, the first thing to go is your peace. Give yourself a carnality check. A stop in church attendance and studying the Word of

Morning Glory

God usually indicate that you're headed down the wrong path. What you're doing is walking in carnality. Change your direction quickly and get back into the Spirit of God where you'll find life and peace.

Therefore if any man be in Christ, he is a new creature: old things are passed away; behold, all things are become new. 2 Cor. 5:17

When you go from carnal to spiritual, old things are passed away and all things become new. The way you walk, talk, dress, work on your job, and even clean your house becomes new. You are new in Christ Jesus and are no longer operating under the law of sin or death. When you're operating under the law of death, you do it with anger because your spirit wants to die. Although you may be fighting to live, you lack the power of God that enables you to live in Him.

Because the carnal mind is enmity against God: for it is not subject to the law of God, neither indeed can be. Romans 8:7

A carnal mind is an enemy to God. When operating in carnality, you begin to hate the Lord and the things He blesses you with. If God blessed you with a new house, you'd live in it and would never invite the saints over because when you hate Him, you also hate His people. You'd take the job God blessed you with, cash your paycheck, and steal His tithes because your mind is set against Him. If the Lord told you to spend quiet time with Him and turn off the TV for seven days, you'd just cringe and say, "It doesn't take all of

that. That's just a bunch of religious mess. I'm not in bondage anymore; the Lord has made me free." Okay, be free then . . . free to go straight to hell!

> *For, brethren, ye have been called unto liberty; only use not liberty for an occasion to the flesh, but by love serve one another.*
>
> Galatians 5:13

See, some people have become so liberated until their freedom has taken them straight back to the bondage of sin. You can't go by what the masses are doing; peer pressure is an old trick of the enemy. When the devil doesn't want you to be purified, he'll even have you join a ministry where everyone else is just as impure as you are so that your spirit can be comfortable in your mess.

Grow up today in the Lord. When you grew up in the natural, you put away childish things; you grew out of playing with Ken and Barbie. Likewise, when you mature in the Lord, there are some things you should just grow out of. You won't have time for the soap operas or sitting there watching people hugging, kissing, and using profanity on TV. You would want to protect yourself and the Holy Spirit that dwells within your temple from being contaminated by carnality.

The Lord desires that you stay sober and be vigilant, not numb to the devil's devices. You don't have to be sifted as wheat. The enemy doesn't have to devour you, but you've got to use an effective strategy. To be a mighty warrior of the Lord, my friend, start abandoning all carnality.

This morning, start testing your spiritual level. For the next week, examine the things that you're involved in by writing down all of your activities. The activities you engage in will let you know where you are spiritually or where you are carnally. Whatever your flesh is attached to usually indicates your spiritual level in the Lord. Today is the day to slay your carnal ways.

GOING AFTER THE CHIEF

For many, the enemy has been lodged in the seat of their soul for so long until he's not ready to give up his residence just because they say, "Get out of here, Satan." Some transcending spirits will flee, but they extend to a master spirit. For instance, if you're unmarried and decided to stop kissing any and everybody, that's good, but you still didn't attack lust—you only stopped kissing. You didn't wound the chief; you just stopped the symptom.

In warfare, you are always required to kill the chief. It is the chief that has the power to regroup and will not only survive, but will also assemble another army to challenge you yet again. So, if all you're doing is attacking the symptoms, then you're not waging a good war. Get to the level of anointing where it's strong enough to purify you against that strong man. You've got to purge if you're going after the chief. The residue of the world may still be on you, and to remove it, undergo a purification process.

But who may abide the day of his coming? and who shall stand when he appeareth? for he is like a refiner's fire, and like fullers' sope: And he shall sit as a refiner and purifier of silver: and he shall purify the sons of Levi, and purge them as gold and silver, that they may offer unto the LORD an offering in righteousness. Malachi 3:2-3

The operation of a fuller is connected to being purged. During Old Testament times, a fuller would get a bucket, fill it with water, and then fill that bucket with clothes. In order to thoroughly cleanse the clothes, he'd have people stomp, beat, and trample the clothes until every trace of dirt and residue was gone. In a spiritual sense, the bucket is symbolic of your temple (body), the water is symbolic of the Holy Spirit, and the clothes are symbolic of your lifestyle. All of those things must be purged if you are going to live holy and be victorious.

Purging is a harsh cleansing; therefore, you're going to feel some pain. When you cease from sinning, realize that you may miss whatever it is you are purging out—be it a dead relationship, cigarettes, giving people a piece of your mind, etc. You are being purged and that thing is being ripped, torn, and stomped out of you.

> *Behold, I give unto you power to tread on serpents and scorpions, and over all the power of the enemy: and nothing shall by any means hurt you. Luke 10:19*

The Lord said He has given you the power to tread. Through the power of the Holy Ghost, you can tread on serpents, scorpions, every evil work of the devil, and all of his power. Don't just sit there wishing the enemy would leave. Tread!

"Well, I just want you to pray for me; I want you to lay hands on me so that God will stop me from lying."

NO! The Word says, "Behold, I give unto you power." You need to get up out of that bed in the morning and start treading and stomping that thing out. Pick yourself up. Get your flesh out of that bed and enter into prayer. Stay in prayer until the Lord immerses you in the Spirit. Then, take the Word of God—the Sword of the Spirit—and cut out all of the filth and junk that has taken a hold of your life.

There's no time to stay up to the wee hours of the morning watching HBO, Showtime, and Nick-at-Night. You're going to have to begin to discipline yourself and set a time schedule. Sometimes, you'll just have to say, "Everyday at 7 o'clock, don't call me. I've got to hurry up in the store and get home, because 7:00 is my purging hour."

If a man therefore purge himself from these, he shall be a vessel unto honour, sanctified, and meet for the master's use, and prepared unto every good work. Flee also youthful lusts: but follow righteousness, faith, charity, peace, with them that call on the Lord out of a pure heart. But foolish and unlearned questions avoid, knowing that they do gender strifes. And the servant of the Lord must not strive; but be gentle unto all men, apt to teach, patient, In meekness instructing those that oppose themselves; if God peradventure will give them repentance to the acknowledging of the truth; And that they may recover themselves out of the snare of the devil, who are taken captive by him at his will. 2 Tim. 2:21-26

If you are tempted and should fall—not out of self-willed, deliberate sin, but if you are ensnared in a trap of the devil and are overtaken in a sin and fall—then due to your level of purification, there should be enough power in you to recover yourself. Don't keep calling the prayer lines with nonsense, saying, "Excuse me . . . Umm, this is Sister Wanna-sin. Well . . . my ex-boyfriend stopped by, and I don't know how we ended up in bed together, but we sort of fell into sin, and I just want you to pray for me."

No. Hang up the phone and recover yourself! I know that may seem a tad harsh, but this book is not for babies. I don't have time to hand feed you or give you pacifiers in this devotional. I have to give it to you straight and tell the truth anyhow. There is no need for you to stay broken down, busted, and disgusted when God has already empowered you to tread. Don't run into hiding and miss services because you fall. Recover. Don't stop praying. Recover! If you quit and give in to guilt, don't you know you're just setting yourself up for that condemnation chief to take up residence in you? Be resilient and recover yourself.

The steps of a good man are ordered by the LORD: and he delighteth in his way. Though he fall, he shall not be utterly cast down: for the LORD upholdeth him with his hand. Psalm 37:23-24

Don't give up—it's not over. Though you may have fallen, the Lord has not utterly cast you down. You're being purified. You keep dealing with certain issues because that's your strong man. Your strong man is the area that you always mess up in. It's your numero uno chief. When it exposes itself, let

God work that thing out and go after that chief.

The Bible says:

> . . . *how can one enter into a strong man's house, and spoil his goods, except he first bind the strong man? and then he will spoil his house. Matthew 12:29*

If you are really serious about knocking out that strong man, then hit it with the one/two punch of fasting and prayer. By not feeding your flesh, you weaken it. It becomes so weak that it can hardly raise its head. While in that state, you should especially strengthen your spirit man by feeding it the Word of God. Then, when that chief tries to resurface again, your spirit will be strong, rise up like a mighty giant, and tower over your flesh.

> *Is not this the fast that I have chosen? to loose the bands of wickedness, to undo the heavy burdens, and to let the oppressed go free, and that ye break every yoke? Isaiah 58:6*

Stop focusing on the symptoms and go after the chief this morning.

Morning Glory

HAVING A RECEPTIVE HEART

If your heart is not in a receptive state, it will continue to be in that same unreceptive state when it comes to receiving from the Lord. You've been so used to guarding yourself from people that you've ended up guarding yourself from the Lord too. Soul ties, childhood issues, and a whole host of things have contributed to erecting hardened walls within your heart—only those same walls can sometimes keep God out.

"Well, I've been hurt so much that I'm not letting anyone get close to my heart. It's not anybody's business what I'm going through anyway. In fact, I'm just tired of people. I'm not going to church. I'll go when the Lord tells me to go. I'm open to God; I'm just not dealing with people."

If that's your attitude, you're shutting down your spirit. When you get like that, the Lord will bind up everything you've got because you're battling with a spirit of pride.

And he shall spread forth his hands in the midst of them, as he that swimmeth spreadeth forth his hands to swim: and he shall bring down their pride together with the spoils of their hands. Isaiah 25:11

Have you ever seen people that used to have a good job and used to have a nice car, but they are still living in yesteryear? They usually stand around saying things like, "That's alright. God is going to give it all back to me. I remember when I had suits to give away. I remember I had shoes everywhere. Everywhere you looked, I had . . ."

Well, they don't have those things anymore!

"I'm not used to asking anybody for anything. I'm independent; I do everything myself. If God doesn't do it for me, then it will not get done. I make my own way. I just get on that bus and go."

You know what? It could be thundering and lightening outside, and because of their silly pride, they won't pick up the phone to ask a friend for a ride. Instead, pride will have them invest $100 in a pair of sneakers and keep on walking in their own personal marathon.

Pride goeth before destruction, and an haughty spirit before a fall.
Proverbs 16:18

If you're not careful, pride can be so strong that it won't even let you ask for or accept prayer.

"Brother, do you need . . ."

"No. I've got this. I'll work it out by myself. I know what I have to do. I don't need you to do a thing for me. I . . . I . . . I . . ."

Two months down the line, you're back in the same old state. You need to understand that your deliverance is connected to someone else, whether you like it or not. I don't care who you are, somebody has your victory right in his or her mouth.

Pride will even keep you from good relationships.

"Well, I got hurt."

So what, get over it. Relationships aren't always rosy. It is pride that says, "I don't want to have anything else to do with you. Once you hurt me like that, I'm through with you. Don't talk to me; don't say anything to me. As a matter of fact, don't even look my way."

Pride is only concerned with protecting you. It doesn't want you to expose yourself; it doesn't want you to admit when you're wrong. It only shows you how everyone else is wrong, not you. You can only focus on what they did to you and said about you. It's always them—never yourself. When you're broken for the Lord's service, you learn to forgive; you learn to examine your own heart, faults, weaknesses, and shortcomings.

You've got to get yourself to a place where you say, "God, if you want to use a dog to bark my way out, I'll appreciate it. I need help; I need a breakthrough. I don't care who you use."

Maybe you haven't gotten there yet. Perhaps you haven't been bound up enough. When you really get messed up and tired of being bound up in your spirit, you won't care who God uses—White, Black, Asian, or Hispanic . . . it will not matter, just as long as the Lord uses them. You'll crave victory.

If you allow it, pride will make you stop reading this devotional because you'll think you know it all anyway. It will cause you to distrust the Lord and only trust in your own mind.

Morning Glory

Let not mercy and truth forsake thee: bind them about thy neck; write them upon the table of thine heart: So shalt thou find favour and good understanding in the sight of God and man. Trust in the LORD with all thine heart; and lean not unto thine own understanding. In all thy ways acknowledge him, and he shall direct thy paths. Be not wise in thine own eyes: fear the LORD, and depart from evil. Proverbs 3:3-7

If you want a receptive heart this morning, dismantle pride. Lean and depend on God—not on your own intellect.

Devotional

Morning Glory

KEEPING A MADE UP MIND

God is not a man, that he should lie; neither the son of man, that he should repent: hath he said, and shall he not do it? or hath he spoken, and shall he not make it good? Numbers 23:19

Do you know that God does not go back on His Word? Once He answers you in prayer, that settles it. The devil cannot stop God. When the Lord tells you "yes" concerning something, the devil knows that he can no longer mess with that situation, because the Word of the Lord has already gone forth. So, what is Satan's next recourse and next mode of attack? Your belief. He is out to sway your belief and trust in the proclaimed Word of God over your situation.

While the manifestation of God's Word for your life is in transit, the devil tries to jump into your circumstances and, more importantly, your mind. The decisions you make during this critical phase are what actually determine whether or not you'll receive God's promise. If you fail to receive the promise of the Lord, then know that it is only because you changed your mind; God did not change.

The enemy loves to create doubt in your mind. The minute you think that your miracle will not manifest, you are setting

the devil up to steal it right from under you. In fact, you're giving it to him wrapped up nice and sweet in a neat little box of unbelief. You just lost the devil's game of trick or treat, only you got tricked and he still got your treat.

The Lord wants us to become so rooted and grounded in His Word that we have the kind of faith and belief that is unmoved by circumstances. A lot of us have lost out on too many promises by following our emotions rather than the infallibility of God's Word and promises. We get all bent out of shape over the things that we see instead of building up our faith and hope to trust the Lord for the things unseen. As soon as our situation starts looking bleak, we start spewing out words of unbelief.

Death and life are in the power of the tongue: and they that love it shall eat the fruit thereof. Proverbs 18:21

No matter how much you consecrate, if you do not control your words, you will kill your blessing every time. God will be saying, "Yes," but you'll be busy saying, "No," so now you're in disagreement with God.

Can two walk together, except they be agreed? Amos 3:3

How can you walk with God, yet still disagree with Him at the same time? If God told you that you can do all things through Christ who strengthens you, and you're still talking about you don't know if you're going to make it, then evidently you are in disagreement with the Lord and His Word.

O generation of vipers, how can ye, being evil, speak good things? for out of the abundance of the heart the mouth speaketh. A good man out of the good treasure of the heart bringeth forth good things: and an evil man out of the evil treasure bringeth forth evil things. But I say unto you, That every idle word that men shall speak, they shall give account thereof in the day of judgment. For by thy words thou shalt be justified, and by thy words thou shalt be condemned. Matthew 12:34-37

Sometimes, we'll get on our knees to pray, and although our heart is saying one thing, our mouths are saying something else. We even get upset and say, "Well, the Lord already knows my heart anyway." If all you needed to rely on was your heart, then the Lord wouldn't have been so specific when He said that death and life are in the power of your tongue—not in what you wished for but lacked the faith to believe.

But let him ask in faith, nothing wavering. For he that wavereth is like a wave of the sea driven with the wind and tossed. For let not that man think that he shall receive any thing of the Lord. A double minded man is unstable in all his ways. James 1:6-8

If your heart is saying one thing and your mouth is saying something else, you are double-minded. Your heart wants one thing, but your mouth keeps killing it. You keep switching back and forth between the two, because you are wavering and unstable. You may hear somebody preach a message and say, "Oh, I know that is for me, Lord. I claim it,

receive it, and decree it right now! Thank You, Lord." Then two days later, there you are saying, "I'm tired of waiting. It's never going to come to pass. I didn't think it was going to happen anyway." Well, you said it, not God. You only spoke out the unbelief, doubt, and lack of faith that was already within your heart.

Keeping a made up mind is a decision you must make and a cross you must bear daily. You must decide to speak words of life and not words of death over the things God has promised you. Walking by faith and not by sight has got to be more than just a cute cliché for you; it must become a way of life. Speak confessions of faith instead of confessions of fear. Stop swaying and watch what you say. Stand strong in His Word today.

Devotional

LOOK OUT AS FAR AS YOUR EYES CAN SEE

The kind of anointing that's available to you today is not charted by the calendar. It is charted by the promises of God. If you are a seed of Abraham, your breakthrough is coming just because of who you are. It does not matter how much you speak in tongues or praise the Lord. The only proof that what you've got is not just in your emotions is the operation of the seed of Abraham in your life. The seed of Abraham comes guaranteed with blessings.

Be encouraged today. You're getting ready to receive some things as a direct result of your bloodline. When you come into the realization that you are the seed of Abraham and that it's already in your blood, it will just come to pass. You don't have to turn your plate down to get a house, and you don't have to go on a consecration to get a car. It's already part of your inheritance and is in your blood.

And the LORD appeared unto him the same night, and said, I am the God of Abraham thy father: fear not, for I am with thee, and will bless thee, and multiply thy seed for my servant Abraham's sake. Genesis 26:24

Some things will be released to you not for your sake, but

for Abraham's sake. Your head may be as hard as a rock at times, but the Lord will bless you anyway because of His promise to Abraham. Perhaps you're saying, "God, I don't even deserve this. I don't know why You're doing this for me. I feel so bad, because I know I haven't been all that I should be. I haven't consecrated or fasted, and I have no idea why You're blessing me like this. Why, Lord?" Because you are the seed of Abraham. Though you may be stubborn at times, never forget your true heritage. You are not perfect and will not always get it right, but you are still the seed of Abraham.

Line up your lineage to the Word of God today. Awaken your spirit to the fact that you are indeed Abraham's seed. When you asked the Lord to forgive you and you accepted the Lord Jesus Christ as your Savior, you became a part of Abraham's bloodline. The Holy Spirit stepped in and gave you a spiritual blood transfusion.

And the LORD said unto Abram, after that Lot was separated from him, Lift up now thine eyes, and look from the place where thou art northward, and southward, and eastward, and westward: For all the land which thou seest, to thee will I give it, and to thy seed for ever. And I will make thy seed as the dust of the earth: so that if a man can number the dust of the earth, then shall thy seed also be numbered. Genesis 13:14-16

Begin to speak to the North, the South, the East, and the West and command it to hold not back the harvest of the Lord. This morning, claim your inheritance. God's promise shall cause His blessings to overtake you from every direction. Come on and receive it by faith today. Just like Abraham, look out as far as your eyes can see!

By faith Abraham, when he was called to go out into a place which he should after receive for an inheritance, obeyed; and he went out, not knowing whither he went. Hebrews 11:8

MAKING THE
SECOND DECISION

Do you remember what it was like the first time you were on fire and sold out for the Lord? You were so elated to join the choir, praise team, usher board, or anything else just to serve the Lord. In the midst of your serving, you may have received compliments from your fellow church friends. Deep down in your subconscious mind, you wanted that pat on the back and to be appreciated. That sense of gratification motivated many of you to do what you otherwise would not feel like doing.

Then, there are times when no amount of compliments, thank you's, or accolades mean anything to you. Suddenly, you find yourself asking God, "What's wrong with me? Why don't I possess the joy I used to have? I'm not eager to do this anymore? Lord, remember the time I couldn't wait to get to church? What happened?" The Lord is saying, "You've got to learn how to live out of the second decision."

If the call of God is on your life, then you will reach a point where you've gone to the end of your journey in the natural sense. You've sang the last song that you can sing on this side; you've preached the last message that you can preach on this side; you've played the last instrument that you can play on this side. There comes a time when you're ripe for another word—a word that's hidden and locked inside the mind of God. Your natural mind cannot comprehend this word because the carnal man cannot walk on this side. In order to get to the mind of God, another decision must be made.

God is saying, "Many will preach about it; many will sing about it; many will even shout about it, but only few will walk therein." Only a few of us will go to the other side. Only a few of us have what it takes to cross over. It's crossing over time. There is enough entertainment in the church; it's crossing over time. Anybody can sit down and write a song. Oh, I know this may raise some eyebrows, but just about anyone can get a few Scriptures together and preach a sermon. Yet, another word is hidden in the Lord that's not on the natural page. The Lord has some songs that have never been sung before. He has some messages that have never been preached before. It's waiting for you on the other side. It doesn't meet the natural eye. There is a message beyond the message.

In this hour, demon spirits have been loosed in this land, and it's going to take more than just a funky beat to get people set free. It will take you laying down your life for the gospel's sake. Oh, we fast for three days and think we've laid down our lives. We wake up in the midnight hour, pray a couple of hours, and think we've laid down our lives. But God is saying that there is much more to it than that. He is saying, "You've got to reach the point that when the fiery darts shoot at you, you're still going to spread the good news of the gospel.

When nobody is patting you on your back for a job well done, you're still going to spread the gospel. If you've got to go by yourself with no money in your pocket, you will still spread the gospel. Why? Because you are spreading the gospel as a result of your decision. You're in another realm. You've reached the other side."

Understand something: By virtue of you reading this page, you have to go to the other side. You don't have any other choice. God is saying to you this morning, "I've called you. I've been calling you. That's right. YOU! Will you answer My call?"

Look back on what God has done for you. Don't block out what you were like when He first got a hold of you. You weren't always wrapped in fine suits. You weren't always sitting with a Bible on your lap. Some of you were hooked on drugs, caught up in homosexuality, thought you could never be anything, and didn't have a dime to your name. It was God's grace and mercy that kept you.

Before the time to make the second decision arrives, you'll usually find yourself regressing and wanting to do some of the things you used to do. Some of those old thoughts will pop and make you wonder why you're daydreaming about your past. If you fail to make the second decision, you stand in danger of regressing in the realm of the spirit because your natural man will seek to repeat itself all over again—only this time, you'll end up with seven more demons than you had before.

You've got some decisions to make this morning. What

are you going to do from this moment forward? Are you going on with God, or are you going back to bondage and sin? Are you going to walk where many dwell, or are you going to live where only few tread? Let me tell you, if you do decide to walk on with the Lord and cross over, you may not see your way at first. You'll feel like you're not walking on anything, but the Holy Spirit will rise up and tell you that you're connected to the Creator of all things. You'll feel like nothing can happen to you there, because you're in another realm. On that other side, you'll finally understand what it is to truly live.

You may not realize it this morning, but something is being broken in the spirit. You are being re-birthed today. An eternal yes has been birthed in the womb of your spirit. The will of God is already settled in your life. I don't care what you're doing now; I don't care what you think you're trapped in now, the Lord's will is unfolding in your life. Thank the Lord. No demon can prevail against it, for God is moving obstacles out of your way. Thank Him for taking you to the other side.

Devotional

MORNING GLORY

My voice shalt thou hear in the morning, O LORD; in the morning will I direct my prayer unto thee, and will look up. Psalm 5:3

As you are reading this devotional, God is calling you to commune with Him early in the morning. When you open your eyes in the morning, connect to the beauty of His holiness. Before you speak to another, speak to the Lord first. Commune with Him and enter into His presence. Allow the Lord to penetrate your spirit and get locked into your thoughts.

But I will sing of thy power; yea, I will sing aloud of thy mercy in the morning: for thou hast been my defense and refuge in the day of my trouble. Psalm 59:16

The Lord GOD hath given me the tongue of the learned, that I should know how to speak a word in season to him that is weary: he wakeneth morning by morning, he wakeneth mine ear to hear as the learned. Isaiah 50:4

I know firsthand that committing to early morning prayer and worship will challenge most just like it challenged me, but its rewards will take you to a new level in God. Nobody said that it would be easy—great things usually aren't. Biblical history teaches us that most of the great acts in the Bible were wrought when? In the morning.

And in the morning, rising up a great while before day, he went out, and departed into a solitary place, and there prayed. Mark 1:35

The majority of today's Christians are stuck in mediocrity and are satisfied to do just enough to get by rather than doing what it takes to propel themselves to a greater level in God. It's time to stop playing games and step out of your comfort zone. If you're not challenged, if your life isn't changing for the better, and if you're not growing in the Lord, then you're just wasting your time. God knows that giving up that last bit of sleep will be a press for most of us. Yet, He also knows that when you're after something from Him, you will persevere. Your sacrifice will not be in vain.

Cause me to hear thy loving kindness in the morning; for in thee do I trust: cause me to know the way wherein I should walk; for I lift up my soul unto thee. Psalm 143:8

Early in the morning, you're fresh and untampered with. Before you become entrenched in the cares of this world, distracted by the car horns blowing, upset because the ironing board broke down, and heated because there's no more hot water, hear what the Spirit of the Lord wants to say to you. Give God the first fruits of your mind before your spouse gets it, before your children get it, before your boss gets it, and before the bill collectors get it. Offer it unto the Lord. Then, when the world hits you and the fire of your trial comes, it will not shake the Word that the Lord spoke to you early that morning. That Word is your manna from heaven.

It will sustain you through anything you'll face that day.

Today's manna is waiting. Yesterday's Word won't be enough to sustain you. Tomorrow has it's own troubles—new levels and new devils. Everyday, you need a fresh Word from the Lord. Get up early and let the Word be the first thing that feeds your spirit. Commit yourself to early morning worship. Press on to your next spiritual level. Up, up, up. Follow His lead, for He is your Bright and Morning Star. Rise up and bask in His Presence . . . bask in the morning glory.

> *I Jesus have sent mine angel to testify unto you these things in the churches. I am the root and the offspring of David, and the bright and morning star. Rev. 22:16*

"OUR FATHER, WHICH ART IN HEAVEN"

After this manner therefore pray ye: Our Father which art in heaven, Hallowed be thy name. Matthew 6:9

Throughout the Bible, we are admonished to recognize God as the Father, for He is the Producer and Creator of all things. All that you need comes from Him.

A lot of our prayers are held up because we have unknowingly offended the Father. We have disrespected Who He is and His name. How? As soon as we hear the word "father", we get all bent out of shape. We can't get through to God because we never liked our natural father and are still holding things against him. By mere word association, we often try to skip the Father entirely and just go straight to Jesus.

"Me and my daddy just don't get along. We never see eye-to-eye. He has never been any good anyway. I don't have a relationship with him because when I was six and wanted a bike, he embarrassed me. I haven't liked him since then. My father left me and never did anything for me. Do you see this scar right here? That's from when he slapped me down. He didn't have to hit me like that. I don't want anything to do with him. He's just a liar anyway. He lies, lies, lies all the day long. See, I didn't even want to mention how he used to get drunk and would come into my room and touch me. You know I could go on and on about that word *father*. Just let me talk to Jesus and the Holy Spirit."

Holding onto things like that often explains why you cannot trust God. You can't lean on God the Father, because you may never have been able to lean on your natural father. You may have learned that your father was an adulterer and cheated on your mother, and all of that mess remained in your mind and is still connected to the word "father". It causes you to not fully trust God. It's nearly impossible for you to really believe that our heavenly Father is going to love you, take care of you, and treat you well when you've been so mistreated by your natural father. It's difficult for you to rely on the Lord with your whole heart when your heart has been so abused and misused.

This may be hard for you, but you know what? You have to get over it. Release all of that bitterness and unforgiveness, or it is going to hinder your relationship with your heavenly Father. I know it may not be easy, but find your daddy and tell him, "I forgive you". If he's dead, then resolve to forgive him in your heart.

"My father is an alcoholic."

Yes, your father may be an alcoholic, but God isn't.

"My father is locked up."

Yes, he may be incarcerated, but that doesn't mean that God isn't ready to set you free.

Come on. You've got to get this. You can't sit there harboring bitterness and unforgiveness against your natural father and think that you're going to be able to relate completely to your heavenly Father.

Some of your blessings are tied up. You're living right, you're praying, you're fasting, you're not doing anything wrong, but why can't you get it? Because you offended the Father. He's saying, "You're supposed to trust Me to take care of you. I'm your heavenly Father. Lean and depend on Me. I am Jehovah Jireh, your provider. I'm your joy, I'm your peace, and I'm your sustenance."

This morning, please repent for anytime you may have dishonored or disrespected God, the Father. Reconcile the way that you treat Him. Do not hold the sins of your father against God—consciously or unconsciously. Forgive your natural father and mother. There may have been an area that you needed to wall up in order to protect yourself, but trust the Lord and let it go. The Lord wants to love all of you. Don't block Him out. You deserve His love, and He is more than worthy of yours. Give it to Him. He'll never leave you; He'll never forsake you; and He'll never fail you. He is there for you, always.

Fear thou not; for I am with thee: be not dismayed; for I am thy God: I will strengthen thee; yea, I will help thee; yea, I will uphold thee with the right hand of my righteousness. Isaiah 41:10

And thou shalt love the Lord thy God with all thy heart, and with all thy soul, and with all thy mind, and with all thy strength: this is the first commandment. Mark 12:30

OVERCOMING CONDEMNATION

There is therefore now no condemnation to them which are in Christ Jesus, who walk not after the flesh, but after the Spirit. Romans 8:1

This morning, understand that you don't have any business with your head hanging down. You are not a failure, just succeeding roughly. The very fact that you are reading this devotion today is an indication that you didn't completely fail God. If you had failed God, you wouldn't have picked up this book. You wouldn't have the power to lift up your hands to the Lord. Had you totally failed God, no praise would have been able to squeeze out of your mouth. Don't let the devil browbeat you with condemnation every time you fall short. Working out your soul's salvation and coming completely out of sin is a process, not a flash.

Though you may be divorced, you are not a failure. You may have been fired, but you're not finished. Sometimes, when the Lord tells you to move and you don't, He will provoke someone's heart to force you to move in order for Him to ultimately get you blessed. You will never be able to proceed to the next step while still wallowing in the past.

Though he fall, he shall not be utterly cast down: for the LORD upholdeth him with his hand. Psalm 37:24

If you are operating in condemnation because there are still areas in your life that you need to repent of, then do that and turn your back to that sin. You must love yourself and respect yourself and not neglect to forgive yourself. Once you have repented, your sins are forever cast into the sea of forgetfulness. Remind yourself that you are now a new creature in Christ. Press onward, not backward. Walk on in the things of God. Walk in the Spirit. Walk on to your future in Christ. Be transformed by the renewing of your mind, instead of replaying your regrets over and over again all of the time.

For the Lord GOD will help me; therefore shall I not be confounded: therefore have I set my face like a flint, and I know that I shall not be ashamed. Isaiah 50:7

Staying ashamed of your past will bind you up and cause you to be overcome with guilt rather than you being free enough to overcome it by the word of your testimony. Hold your head up, and go on in the Lord. You've come too far to give up now. The devil is the accuser of the brethren and a consummate deceiver. How dare you allow him to declare you unfit for the Master's use. The Lord chose you, died for you, and has forgiven you. Be strong and keep the faith today.

And the great dragon was cast out, that old serpent, called the Devil, and Satan, which deceiveth the whole world: he was cast out into the earth, and his angels were cast out with him. And I heard a loud voice saying in heaven, Now is come salvation, and strength, and the kingdom of our God, and the power of his Christ: for the accuser of the brethren is cast down, which accused them before God day and night. And they overcame him by the blood of the Lamb, and by the word of their testimony; and they loved not their lives unto the death. Revelation 12: 9-11

Morning Glory

OVERCOMING INIQUITY

Iniquity is anything that is thought, said, or acted upon without God being in it.

"I see absolutely nothing wrong with going to see this movie."

Many times did he deliver them; but they provoked him with their counsel, and were brought low for their iniquity. Psalm 106:43

Let me repeat myself: Iniquity is anything that is thought, said, or acted upon without God being in it. If you think that sounds just a tad too strict, fine . . . just watch yourself. If you continually feed your mind and spirit with ungodly things and indulge in activities where there is no trace of God, then you will continually fail God. You will keep battling between your will and the will of the Lord. When He tells you to turn off the TV, you'll say, "Well, I'm just going to watch this one last piece here." When He tells you to wake up and pray, you'll flat out tell Him that you don't feel like it. When He tells you to fast, you'll do the exact opposite and go out and order a huge prime rib and cheesecake instead.

Understand something: The problem doesn't lie in the TV, your sleep, nor in the food that you eat. The problem is wrapped up in that spirit within you that is constantly telling God no. The problem is your disobedience to the Lord.

Wash me thoroughly from mine iniquity, and cleanse me from my sin. Psalm 51:2

I acknowledged my sin unto thee, and mine iniquity have I not hid. I said, I will confess my transgressions unto the LORD; and thou forgavest the iniquity of my sin. Selah. Psalm 32:5

The Lord desires to wash you from your iniquities, but are you just going to dirty yourself up again as soon as the prime-time hour rolls around? The word "Selah" in the Scripture above means "think on this". Do that this morning—give some deep and serious thought to your ways, your sins, and your iniquities. How many times are you going to keep repenting for the same old things? Ask the Lord to cleanse you from all unrighteousness and teach you His ways.

PASS THE TEST

Most of us have heard it said that everything is going to be all right. Well, let me just start off by telling you that everything is not going to be all right. There are some things that you will have to live with; the Lord will not even make them all right for you. Now, I know that may be shocking, but understand that there's something in each and every one of us that we wrestle and battle with.

> *For this thing I besought the Lord thrice, that it might depart from me. And he said unto me, My grace is sufficient for thee: for my strength is made perfect in weakness. Most gladly therefore will I rather glory in my infirmities, that the power of Christ may rest upon me. 2 Cor. 12:8-9*

There's no need in thinking that you are exempt, as though this particular devotion is for everyone else but you. In order to excel in your spiritual walk, first of all, you have to quit fooling yourself; you've got a test to pass just like everyone else. When God sets you completely free from everything forever, you will no longer be on this earth—you'll be heaven!

Consider Job for a moment. Everything that happened to Job, the Lord allowed to happen. In fact, the devil received permission from the Lord to wreak havoc in Job's life; however, the more Job prayed, the more he became God's chosen one. God continually poured His Spirit upon Job. Even when Job was crying out, the Lord was essentially saying, "No. I will not deliver you just yet, because I've got a point to prove to the devil." The trouble with some of us is that we won't allow God to prove His point and win. For instance, if a bill is overdue, instead of begging, pleading, and crying to the Lord, ask Him to teach you what He wants you to learn. Perhaps He's trying to teach you that it's not just money that you need, but you need faith also. He could be teaching you to be disciplined so that you'll stop living above your means. He could also be teaching you that when you rob Him of His tithes and offerings, the devourer has not been rebuked for your sake. Whatever the lesson, learn it and pass the test.

And we know that all things work together for good to them that love God, to them who are the called according to his purpose.

Romans 8:28

"All things are working together for my good. Therefore, I thank You, Lord, because this is not just an affliction; it's my blessing. It is my passage into the Holy of holies. Lord, I shall obey You in this and in all things."

Some people persist in harboring unforgiveness against others and never take note of the lessons God is trying to teach them. When an unforgiving spirit has a stronghold in you, in order for God to expose it, He'll allow certain things to come against you. Once you're aware that unforgiveness still exists in you, pass that test. Don't get caught up in the pettiness of talking about the wrongs that people have committed against you. Begin to ask the Lord to reveal to you the things He wants to cancel out of your life. What is it about you that the He wants to correct?

Therefore I take pleasure in infirmities, in reproaches, in necessities, in persecutions, in distresses for Christ's sake: for when I am weak, then am I strong. 2 Cor. 12:10

Each test is designed to teach you something. When you're weak and beaten down by the cares of life, it is then that the Lord will be strong for you. Learn to depend on Him. When you feel like you're shipwrecked all by yourself and the shore seems nowhere in sight, trust the Lord to be your help and deliverer.

God is our refuge and strength, a very present help in trouble.
Psalm 46:1

The Lord has many characteristics and facets. You not only learn about Him through joy; you learn about Him through affliction as well. Praise the Lord with fervor in spite of your circumstance, for He is still worthy. During moments of suffering, you'll often feel the anointing heavier than ever before. Your praise will be stronger because that suffering is refining something greater in you. Pass the test.

If you keep failing your tests, you'll keep being confronted with them until you finally pass. You can keep changing churches if you want to and move all the way out of town, but whatever spirit you didn't like will just be waiting for you wherever you go. You may sit on a different side of the church, but when God ordains for you to do battle with a spirit, that spirit will keep stalking you; all it has to do is use people for a moment. If you had a problem with someone and you failed your test, that spirit will jump out, seek another available vessel, and test you all over again. If you talk too much, then the Lord will let that spirit jump around until you finally learn how to keep your mouth shut. Eventually, you'll pass the test one way or the other.

For we wrestle not against flesh and blood, but against principali-ties, against powers, against the rulers of the darkness of this world, against spiritual wickedness in high places. Ephesians 6:12

"Well, I was involved with this man, and since I just couldn't stop the relationship, I moved out of town."

Perhaps you need to understand that you weren't just dealing with a man, but with a spirit too. It will find other men to use wherever you go until you pass your test. Another man may have on a different suit and a different tie, but he'll have the same familiar spirit.

If really you want to be delivered, then fast. The Word says:

Is not this the fast that I have chosen? to loose the bands of wicked-ness, to undo the heavy burdens, and to let the oppressed go free, and that ye break every yoke? Isaiah 58:6

Devotional

Die to the demands of your flesh.

Mortify therefore your members which are upon the earth; fornication, uncleanness, inordinate affection, evil concupiscence, and covetousness, which is idolatry: Col. 3:5

Meditate on the Lord and His Word and fail not to speak words of life. Refrain from speaking negativity and words of death over your situation.

This book of the law shall not depart out of thy mouth; but thou shalt meditate therein day and night, that thou mayest observe to do according to all that is written therein: for then thou shalt make thy way prosperous, and then thou shalt have good success. Joshua 1:8

In order to test your level of obedience to God, you're going to have to go through some trials. Stop making excuses for the issues you've been dealing with for a while; just pass the test. You already know the warning signs for some things, so heed them. Graduate to your next level in God. Pass the test today, my friend. Pass the test.

PERSONAL TRAINING

Behold, I was shapen in iniquity; and in sin did my mother conceive me. Psalm 51:5

Remember: We weren't born God, Jr. We were born in sin and shaped in iniquity; therefore, some of the issues that we're dealing with right now have been embedded in us since we were children. When Jesus enters our lives, He has to break off our old nature daily. The residue from the world needs to be broken off of us every single day. When you say or do things that are off kilter, you shouldn't condemn yourself for it, because that thing is about to be broken out of your life; it needed to be exposed in order to be destroyed.

Saying, Father, if thou be willing, remove this cup from me: nevertheless not my will, but thine, be done. And there appeared an angel unto him from heaven, strengthening him. And being in an agony he prayed more earnestly: and his sweat was as it were great drops of blood falling down to the ground. Luke 22:42-44

When you prefer the will of the Lord to your own, you know that the Holy Spirit lives in you. When Jesus was in the garden, He wasn't arguing with the Holy Spirit. Instead, Jesus submitted Himself as the Son to the Father, so that He could train us how to be submitted to the Holy Spirit, in order for us to get to the Father through the Son. Got it?

The Holy Spirit is like out personal trainer. When Jesus was born through Mary, He already knew that He had to be trained. He submitted to whatever the Trainer told Him to do; He stayed as long as he was told to stay; He went where He was told to go; He also only touched what He was told to touch. If we are to ever have the mind of Christ, then we must also avail ourselves to that same training. Being born in the natural is being made to live. Being born in the spiritual sense means to chose to die. You willfully chose to die to your self, and live in God. To live in the presence of the Lord, you've got to take up your cross and follow Him. It's time to take your death walk.

Jesus said:

For my yoke is easy, and my burden is light. Matthew 11:30

Your cross is lighter than you think, so pick it up and let's go!

PRAY ACCORDING TO THE LORD'S WILL

God is not shocked by anything that you ask Him for. Whether or not He grants your request depends on if you've asked for something that's already in His will. If you're praying in your flesh, then you haven't tapped the mind or the will of God. Until you allow the Lord to purify the deeds of your flesh, you will continually pray for fleshly desires to be fulfilled.

"I want to get married. Lord, I thank You because You told me that I can just describe what I want. I've heard people say that I need to be more detailed, so, here it is: I want a tall, dark, and handsome man. I want him to have a good job, preferably in my industry. I want him to drive a Lexus and have a Jeep. He should have at least 5 Armani suits, but don't let him mix them up with Versace shirts, Lord. I want him to already have a mansion in . . ."

Now, what if the Lord is saying that He doesn't have a husband for you right now, but instead He's sending you to China to be a missionary? In order to receive that, your flesh has got to die. Do you really want His will, or do you only want what will bring you prestige, honor, glamour, and glory?

Some singles need to get like me. "Lord, I don't care where he comes from. If my husband-to-be doesn't have any teeth,

I know a great dentist that can help him up out. No clothes?
That's okay—we can go shopping. Just send him, Lord!"

I know that may sound funny, but understand the principle behind it. We cannot limit what God may have for us.
When God sends a blessing our way, it would be a shame to
miss it because of being stuck on superficial things. I'd rather
have a toothless man any day than a handsome drunk beating
me down every time I turned around. I'd rather have happi-
ness with someone that didn't quite fit my ideal "image" of a
husband than be miserable with someone that looked good
on the outside but was rotten to the core. The Lord's will is to
supply all of my needs. Well, I need joy, not misery; I need
integrity, not sexy; I need character, not a charmer; I need
peace, and not drama.

> *Let the wicked forsake his way, and the unrighteous man his
> thoughts: and let him return unto the LORD, and he will have mercy
> upon him; and to our God, for he will abundantly pardon. For my
> thoughts are not your thoughts, neither are your ways my ways,
> saith the LORD. For as the heavens are higher than the earth, so are
> my ways higher than your ways, and my thoughts than your
> thoughts. Isaiah 55:7-9*

Oftentimes, condemnation and guilt can separate us from
the truth of God's Word. It can keep our minds so mired in
the mistakes of our past, that we fail to believe the will of the
Lord for our lives. While we're busy feeling dirty, pitiful, and
ashamed, we forget that God forgave us at the point of our

repentance. It almost seems too good to be true that we serve a God that has cast all of our sins into the sea of forgetfulness. Begin to see yourself as God sees you:

Therefore if any man be in Christ, he is a new creature: old things are passed away; behold, all things are become new. 2 Cor. 5:17

- You are a new creature in Christ

And hath raised us up together, and made us sit together in heavenly places in Christ Jesus: Ephes. 2:6

- You have been raised up

No weapon that is formed against thee shall prosper; and every tongue that shall rise against thee in judgment thou shalt condemn. This is the heritage of the servants of the LORD, and their righteousness is of me, saith the LORD. Isaiah 54:17

- No weapon formed against you shall prosper

Neither shall they say, Lo here! or, lo there! for, behold, the kingdom of God is within you. Luke 17:21

- The kingdom of God is within you

Behold, I give unto you power to tread on serpents and scorpions, and over all the power of the enemy: and nothing shall by any means hurt you. Luke 10:19

- You have been empowered

Diligently study the Word of the Lord, and you shall surely know His will. It is not the Lord's will for you to fail; it is not His will for you to be depressed; it is not His will for you to grumble and complain. Know the God you serve, and allow the Spirit of the Lord to reveal to you His will.

Thy kingdom come. Thy will be done in earth, as it is in heaven.
Matthew 6:10

PRAY WITHOUT CEASING

Pray without ceasing. 1 Thes. 5:17

God is calling you to another level in prayer. He wants to teach you how to fight. Pay close attention right now, because anything you want, you're going to have to pray for it. God is saying, "If you want it, come and get it." That's right; if you want it badly enough, you'll go and get it in prayer. You are going to have to pray your way in, and you're going to have to pray your way out.

The car that you drive, you're going to pray to pay it off. The house that you live in, you're going to have to pray it out of the mortgage company. Whatever business you want, you're going to pray your way into it. If your marriage is falling apart, pray until the Lord fixes it. If you don't have a spouse and you know you want to get married, then pray until you get one. If you're about to lose your car, pray to keep and maintain it.

The Lord wants to teach you how to pray. He's designing prayer in your life. God is calling you to a greater walk with Him. If you are not currently rooted in daily, unceasing prayer, then start out by giving the Lord at least seven minutes a day. God will birth a new level of prayer in you, but you have to be consistent and make it a daily part of your life. Prayer needs to become so ingrained in you that it's just as essential as waking up in the morning and brushing your teeth.

Pray at the bus stop. Pray on the plane. Pray in the car. Pray on your job. Pray, pray, pray all the day long. Don't stop praying. When you're in your car, turn the radio off and pray. I don't care if you are listening to Christian music; there's a time to turn it off. There's even a time to turn off the preaching tapes because your flesh needs to hear you praying. You'd be surprised at how the power of God will use your own voice to shake up things in the spirit realm.

Don't ever underestimate the power of prayer. Start praying about everything.

"Can you come over?"

"Let me pray about it."

"I want you to go with me to this event."

"I have to pray about it."

"Can you loan me some money?"

"I have to take it to the Lord in prayer first."

Your answer awaits you in prayer. God said, "Come and get it." If you want peace, then walk in prayer. If it's joy that you want, then walk in prayer.

Get used to walking around your house and praying.

"Hallelujah. I bless you, Lord."

"What are you doing?"

"Praying to keep the lights on; praying to keep the gas on; praying that they don't turn the phone off today; praying that they give me some more time to pay my rent; praying that I don't get fired."

"Man, what are you doing?"

"Praying."

"What are you praying about?"

"I'm praying that I don't fail God today. I feel hot in my flesh; I've got to pray."

You're reading this today because you are at a point in your life where you cannot afford to tiptoe in the flesh. You cannot afford to be sticking your head outside of the will of God. Every time you step out of His will, you're losing time. Every time you wander away from the Lord, you miss out on things. When you live in the Spirit, it's as though you are traveling through light years. God may have promised you a car this year, but when you stepped out of the Spirit for that 20-minute thrill, a year passed you by. I'm talking about spiritual things right now. You're accomplishing things that you never thought you could, because the Holy Ghost has you on a fast track in the Spirit. He's shooting you past every thing that's in opposition to you.

When you step off into fleshly desires, you step off in time. What seems like 15 minutes in the natural is actually years in the spirit. By the time you get back on the right track, you've missed your promise, and you've got to wait and start all over again. Some of you will never get married because you keep stepping out into your flesh. While you are busy fondling and feeling somebody up, you're missing the blessing God has for you. That's deep. Have you ever thought about that?

How many things have you missed just by jumping off into your flesh for a few minutes? How many prophecies haven't come to pass? How many times are you going to have to start over?

Stay on track and stay in the Spirit, and pray without ceasing.

PRAYER OF ASKING

And whatsoever ye shall ask in my name, that will I do, that the Father may be glorified in the Son. John 14:13

The Lord will do whatsoever you ask once your flesh has been purged. If you ask for something ungodly in His name, the Lord is not going to grant that desire. Maybe, just maybe, you should check out the latter part of the verse above — "that the Father may be glorified in the Son". Most of the things people ask God for are not about to bring one ounce of glory to the Father or the Son. Most of the things they ask for is to only glorify themselves.

Ye ask, and receive not, because ye ask amiss, that ye may consume it upon your lusts. James 4:3

When the Lord gets you into the realm of the Spirit and reveals what His will is for you, then you can open up your mouth to ask anything, because you are going to pray for what is already in the Lord's will. Come on; you've got to be in Him in order to be able to ask in His name in the first place. When you ask for something that's in the will of the Lord, you will not ask amiss.

If you are a babe in Christ, you're not expected to automatically know the Lord's will—you're not familiar enough

with Him yet; you haven't been in His presence long enough;
you haven't seen His actions long enough to know His
personality; therefore, you have to ask Him, and then wait to
see if He answers you. Ask the Lord to help you walk in His
will. Don't beat yourself over the head just because you don't
know everything about Him yet—that's a normal part of
growing up in the Lord.

Be encouraged today. Once you know God, you'll know
that it's not His will for you to be sick, but well. You'll know
that by His stripes, you're already healed. You'll know that
God will supply all of your needs according to His riches in
glory, then you can say, "Satan, take your hands off of my
money. I speak prosperity into my life and bind up poverty,
in Jesus' name. I loose the spirit of wealth into every area of
my life."

Thank the Lord for His will this morning. Thank Him for
revealing Himself to you. Thank Him for the times when you
didn't quite know Him, but He came through for you
anyhow. Thank Him for enlightening you to His ways,
because He could have left you in the dark; He never had to
bring you into His marvelous light. The knowledge you have
of Christ wasn't always there. He's been so good to you.
Thank the Lord, for He's worthy. Study His Word and His
ways so that you can graduate from the prayer of asking to
praying according to His will. Allow the Lord to teach and
train you to know His will today.

Morning Glory

PRAYER OF INTERCESSION

When you are in prayer for someone and pleading on their behalf, you are in the prayer of intercession. True intercessors leave personal feelings aside and will earnestly pick up the burden of the Lord. The purpose of prayer is to know what God knows, to feel what He feels, and to respond to His purpose. Until we begin to see as He sees, we will not be able to sense the true need to pray. There are some people that the Lord wants to move you to intercede for, but if you're judgmental, you will turn a deaf ear to the Lord's beckoning.

But when he saw the multitudes, he was moved with compassion on them, because they fainted, and were scattered abroad, as sheep having no shepherd. Matthew 9:36

Jesus was moved with compassion because he felt the burden; He saw the need. If the Lord wants you to pray for drug addicts, you may not be able to sense their burden if you only stay cooped up in your house all of the time. Sometimes you've got to get out your house, walk down the street, and go where they are.

When you are ready for intercession, you will not see people as problems; you'll see the problem in the person's spirit. True intercessors don't walk around holding grudges. They can love a person that just lied on them five minutes ago, because they recognize that person is struggling with a lying spirit. An intercessor is able to discern that the enemy uses people but for a moment. Why wrestle against the person when the spirit that's in them is the real root of the problem?

For we wrestle not against flesh and blood, but against principalities, against powers, against the rulers of the darkness of this world, against spiritual wickedness in high places. Ephes. 6:12

Before you even get to the level of intercession, the first thing you have to learn how to do is keep your mouth shut. If God allows you to feel somebody's burden, don't go blabbing their business all around town. You've got to be loyal and trustworthy.

Now, if your prayer life only centers on yourself, you may become a strong prayer warrior, but you'll never be an intercessor. How can you pick up the burden of the Lord when you're always busy picking up your own? To be an intercessor, you've got to know how to cast all of your cares on Him. Jesus said:

For my yoke is easy, and my burden is light. Matthew 11:30

Dear friend, you are reading this devotion today because the Lord is calling you to another level in prayer. There are some things the Lord wants you to intercede for in order to break in your church, in your home, and among your family

and friends. There are some people He wants you to intercede for that you don't even know, but you have to yield
yourself totally to the Lord. The Lord wants all of you—your
spirit, heart, mind, soul, body, and strength. Sell out
completely. Don't half-step. There are too many people that
you need to pray through certain situations. Too many of
your loved ones are still hell-bound. Don't stop praying when
you've covered yourself; pick up the burden of the Lord this
morning and also intercede for someone else.

Confess your faults one to another, and pray one for another, that ye
may be healed. The effectual fervent prayer of a righteous man
availeth much. James 5:16

Morning Glory

PRAYER OF PRAISE

Praise ye the LORD. Praise God in his sanctuary: praise him in the firmament of his power. Praise him for his mighty acts: praise him according to his excellent greatness. Praise him with the sound of the trumpet: praise him with the psaltery and harp. Praise him with the timbrel and dance: praise him with stringed instruments and organs. Praise him upon the loud cymbals: praise him upon the high sounding cymbals. Let every thing that hath breath praise the LORD. Praise ye the LORD. Psalm 150:1-6

I will bless the LORD at all times: his praise shall continually be in my mouth. Psalm 34:1b

When you offer praise unto the Lord, you glorify Him. You are commending Him because He is worthy. Praise isn't just a bunch of fluffy hymns; sometimes, it is your survival tool. If you're defeated in your spiritual life, then you won't be able to make it in the natural. How are you going to have strength to work on your job when you don't even have enough strength to praise God for five minutes? Praise ye the Lord! The devil isn't standing back like a little, scary cat. He has unleashed his forces to constantly oppose you; dismantle his forces with your praise. Sometimes, you just need to ball up your fists, get in the trenches, and praise your way out.

"Father, we thank You, we glorify You, and we give Your name the praise. We give You the honor and the glory. We lift You up, exalt, and magnify You today. You are the King of kings and the Lord of lords. There is none like You, God. We praise You because we know that in spite of what the world is doing, You are still on the throne. We recognize You this morning to be our Sovereign God.

Lord, we praise You for being the God of our salvation. We praise You for being El Shaddai. We praise You, God, for being more than enough. We praise You because You're honorable, You're high, and You are lifted up. You have so much depth that nobody can go under You; You're too high for anything to go above You; You're too wide for anything to go around You. We glorify You for Your utter awesomeness!

Lord, we thank You right now. We even thank You for the temptation, for we know You've made our way of escape. We thank You for the test, for we know that You are teaching us, and as long as we stay in You, we will not fail. We thank You for the tribulation, for we know that You designed it, and we trust that You are bringing us out. We know Satan cannot touch us without Your permission, and You will not give us more than we can bear. We give Your name the praise, because You said in Your Word that all things work together for the good to them that love You, and those who are called according to Your purpose. We love and adore You, Lord, and we recognize our call this morning. We've gotten to know who we are, and we recognize that we are the called, chosen, and selected ones. Our purpose is in You, Lord. We know You've orchestrated our lives, and we give You the praise today.

You said in Your Word that You shall supply all of our needs according to Your riches in glory. We praise You for our needs being met, because today, oh God, we need a miracle; we need a breakthrough; we need our hearts to be mended; we need to be revived, refreshed, and restored; we need to be washed and thoroughly cleansed from all unrighteousness. We praise You, Lord, for where there's a need, there's also a supplier. We thank You right now for being Jehovah Jireh. You are our Provider.

We praise You this morning for being Jehovah Shalom, our Peace. We praise You for peace in the midst of confusion. We praise You for peace in the midst of trouble. We praise You for the kind of peace that surpasses all understanding. The world doesn't understand Your peace; according to their standards, we should still be crying and depressed. Lord, we praise You right now, for the joy of the Lord is our strength.

We praise You today because Your anointing destroys the yokes in our lives. We praise You because even when we thought we would fail, You made us more than conquerors through Christ Jesus Who loved us. You alone are able to keep us from falling and present us faultless before Your presence with exceeding joy. Hallelujah! We praise You, Lord, for greater is He that is in us than he that is in the world. Lord, You have made us victorious, and we praise You for the victory this morning. Be magnified and exalted today, Lord. In Jesus' name. Amen."

PRAYER OF THANKSGIVING

Enter into his gates with thanksgiving, and into his courts with praise: be thankful unto You, and bless his name. Psalm 100:4

When you enter into the Lord's presence, thank Him first. Giving thanks expresses your appreciation and gratitude to Him. Tell the Lord that you love and adore Him. Thank Him for Who He is and all that He's already done. Let Him know that if He doesn't do anything else, He's already done more than enough. Thank Him, and then you can enter into:

Casting all your care upon him; for he careth for you. 1 Peter 5:7

When we neglect to thank the Lord, but, instead, engage in a begging festival, I wonder if the Lord just sits back saying:

"You want what? Thank Me for what I've already done for you first, with your selfish self. I woke you up this morning and started you on your way. I've been good to you. Is your idea of gratitude coming before me whining and talking about, 'Well, You know the phone bill is due, Grandma's sugar is up, Daddy's blood pressure is sky-high again, and my check is short?' Is that all you can muster up to say to Me? Am I just a dumpster for your never-ending list of needs? Who am I to you, Santa Claus?"

Remember: God is a spirit and He has a character, personality, and feelings too. Thank Him and lift Him up.

In every thing give thanks: for this is the will of God in Christ Jesus concerning You. 1 Thes. 5:18

Be careful for nothing; but in every thing by prayer and supplication with thanksgiving let Your requests be made known unto God. Philip. 4:6

"Lord, You told us to enter into Your gates with thanksgiving, and into Your courts with praise. So, we come before Your presence right now with our hearts full of thanks, love, and praise for You.

Father, all glory, all honor, and all power belong to You— hallowed be Thy name. You are our God; You are our King; You are our Master—our everything; You are our Messiah, our risen Savior, and our Lord. We thank You, God, for sitting on the heavenly throne with authority, power, and dominion over the earth. Thank You for being Alpha and Omega—You are our beginning, and You are our end. Hallelujah!

We thank You for life, we thank You for our health, and we thank You for our strength today. We thank You because You alone are our way out of no way. Thank You for giving Your Son, Jesus, the power to redeem us back to You. Thank You for the plan of salvation and for interceding on our behalf. If we had 10,000 tongues, we couldn't thank You enough.

Lord, because of Your deity and character, we are not lacking in anything. We do not lack joy, we do not lack peace, we do not lack understanding, we don't lack righteousness, grace, or mercy; we don't lack Your everlasting kindness or Your gift of eternal life. We couldn't thank You enough, Lord, for You've been better to us than we've been to ourselves.

Thank You for Your mercy—the kind of mercy that endures forever. When we don't deserve it, You still extend Your mercy, Lord. When we fail You, You still stretch forth mercy. When we fall short of Your will and Your ways, You still offer us Your mercy. When we should have died in our sins and been cursed and cut off, Lord, You were still merciful to us. Your mercy looks beyond all of our faults, and sees our needs.

We thank You for Your presence today, for in Your presence, there is fullness of joy. We thank You for Your anointing today, for it is Your anointing that is breaking and destroying every yoke in our lives. Thank You, Lord, that no weapon formed against us shall prosper—it didn't prosper yesterday, it's not going to prosper today, and it will never prosper in the future.

Lord, we thank You for Your Word, because Your Word never fails, never changes, and will endure from everlasting to everlasting. Thank You for lifting up our burdens, being our protection, our strong tower, and our shield. We thank You in advance for the victory, for the anointing, and for

Your healing power. Thank You for helping us to be longsuf-
fering, because though we may suffer long, we shall not suffer
forever. You are a very present help in a time of need. Lord,
thank You for helping us to endure.

Thank You for enlightening our understanding, increasing
our knowledge, and bestowing Your wisdom upon us. Thank
You that You're washing, cleansing, and purging us . . .
refreshing, renewing, and reviving us . . . justifying, quali-
fying, and equipping us . . . anointing, appointing, and calling
us. Thank You, Father. Thank You, Jesus. Thank You, Holy
Spirit. We cannot sing Your praises enough. Oh Lord, be
exalted this morning. Be magnified on high. Thank You,
Lord. In Jesus' name we pray. Amen."

Morning Glory

PRAYING IN THE NAME OF JESUS

Ye have not chosen me, but I have chosen you, and ordained you, that ye should go and bring forth fruit, and that your fruit should remain: that whatsoever ye shall ask of the Father in my name, he may give it you. John 15:16

Do you know that Jesus is your guarantee? When you pray in His name, you honor Him and recognize the awesome sacrifice He made for you through the shedding of His blood.

Jesus saith unto him, I am the way, the truth, and the life: no man cometh unto the Father, but by me. John 14:6

Jesus is the "Way." You may not be able to see your way out, but look to your Waymaker today. From temptation to death, He's made a way out for you.

There hath no temptation taken you but such as is common to man: but God is faithful, who will not suffer you to be tempted above that ye are able; but will with the temptation also make a way to escape, that ye may be able to bear it. 1 Cor. 10:13

Jesus is the "Truth." Lies are fathered by the devil; God can be no part of that. The root of deception in your life must loosen its grip today. Command it to flee in the name of Jesus. The lie has got to die.

And ye shall know the truth, and the truth shall make you free.
John 8:32

Jesus is the "Life." There is resurrection power in the name of Jesus. Speak life into your mind, life into your body, life into your spirit, life into your emotions, life into your finances, life into your family, life into your church, life into every dead thing in your life that must live. Command it to live this morning, in the name of Jesus. Resurrect it this morning, and command life to come forth, in the matchless name of Jesus.

Jesus said unto her, I am the resurrection, and the life: he that believeth in me, though he were dead, yet shall he live: John 11:25

And these signs shall follow them that believe; In my name shall they cast out devils; they shall speak with new tongues; They shall take up serpents; and if they drink any deadly thing, it shall not hurt them; they shall lay hands on the sick, and they shall recover. Mark 16:17-18

There's healing power in His name. Deliverance is in His name. If you need to be delivered from something this morning, call on that name, Jesus. If you need your body

Devotional

healed, you don't have to go to the Lord explaining the doctor's diagnosis—by His stripes, you are already healed. Call on the name of Jesus. He's given you the power to lay hands on the sick; therefore, use it. Recover yourself. Lay hands on yourself and command that sickness to go. Those symptoms must cease, and your healing must manifest. It's done. It's in His holy name.

You've been given the authority to cast out demons in the name of Jesus. Don't call Satan's name and think you're going to stop him without using Jesus' name. You'll get on your knees and say, "Satan, you know you're a liar, and the truth isn't in you. Amen." The next thing you'll know, your lights are getting turned off, your landlord is acting shady, your supervisor is acting crazy, your house is catching on fire, you're getting into accidents, and all kinds of things will happen. It is only Jesus' name that gives you authority. Like American Express, don't you pray without it.

Back the devil up right now. He has to take his hands off of your stuff. Command it in the name of Jesus. If the enemy is trying to prevail, then you tell him, "The blood of Jesus is against you; it's over the door posts of my life. Flee! In Jesus' name."

That at the name of Jesus every knee should bow, of things in heaven, and things in earth, and things under the earth; Philip. 2:10

PRAYING THROUGH DISTRACTION

There are many people that know the Bible backward and forward, have plenty of information, but still cannot live a word of it. The power of the Word never penetrated their spirit man. That is why we need to be alert and ready when entering into the presence of the Lord. If not, we'll allow the spirit of distraction to block the anointing.

Have you ever been in church and as soon as you sit down, your mind starts wandering to other things? Those thoughts will dance in and out of your mind just when the Lord is trying to penetrate your spirit. Distractions will cause you to completely miss certain things at times.

When you're about to enter into the presence of the Lord, understand that your life is about to be changed. Begin to do battle with your flesh by commanding it to be still; otherwise, it will sit right in the presence of God and tell you about all of the things you should have done today, could have done yesterday, and might not get a chance to do tomorrow. It's nothing but the spirit of distraction trying to get your mind off of what's about to happen in you. Follow Paul's example:

But I keep under my body, and bring it into subjection: lest that by any means, when I have preached to others, I myself should be a castaway. 1 Cor. 9:27

The spirit of distraction really isn't that hard to discern. You try to get comfortable before you pray. You put on your big, cuddly jogging suit and puffy socks, and you situate your pillow just right, then, "Zzzzzzz". Somebody comes in and asks, "Are you sleeping?" You answer, "No, I'm just resting my eyes in the Lord. Zzzzzzz. Huh, oh no, no. I'm not asleep. I'm (yawning) in the spirit. Father, in the name of Jesus . . . Zzzzzzz . . . Umm, thank You, Jesus. Amen."

Let me share my own experience. My first time in intercession, the devil said, "You've got to use the bathroom. You better get up." I said, "I'm not getting up out of this prayer for my bladder or anything else, and I'm not falling asleep. I'll get up and walk around this bedroom, but I'm not coming out of this prayer." So I interceded and prayed, and when I finished, guess what? The bedroom floor was wet! Now the devil knows—don't even go to her with a bladder issue, because she will not be moved!

Begin to notice some of the distractions in your own life. Sometimes, just as you're about to enter into the Lord's presence, your telephone will ring off the hook, and your pager will go off with a 911 emergency code. Urgent? No, it's not urgent—it's a distraction! Learn how to tell people that you're praying. Either invite them to join the prayer or hang up. The devil knows that you're about to come after him and strip him of his power. He knows that if he doesn't stop you with the telephone, if he doesn't stop you with your kidneys, and if he can't even stop you with your bowel movement, then you're really going to tear him up!

Devotional

Who shall separate us from the love of Christ? shall tribulation, or distress, or persecution, or famine, or nakedness, or peril, or sword? As it is written, For thy sake we are killed all the day long; we are accounted as sheep for the slaughter. Nay, in all these things we are more than conquerors through him that loved us. For I am persuaded, that neither death, nor life, nor angels, nor principalities, nor powers, nor things present, nor things to come, Nor height, nor depth, nor any other creature, shall be able to separate us from the love of God, which is in Christ Jesus our Lord. Romans 8:35-39

What shall separate you from the love of Christ? Shall the telephone, pager, fax, weather, television, music, e-mail, internet, arguments, hunger, sickness, family, friends, or your feelings separate you? For your sake, if you're really serious about getting to your next level in God, then you've got to determine right now to let nothing distract or interfere with your time with the Lord. Conquer all of your distractions and stay committed to remaining focused, steadfast, unmovable, and unwavering to the task at hand.

PRAYING WITH AUTHORITY

According to the world's standards, an authority gains influence as a result of acquired information or prestige; however, to be able to issue a command in regard to spiritual matters, one needs much more than mere knowledge. First of all, you must have the right to have authority.

Now, I know that some of you are just raring to assert your authority in the spirit realm and push your weight around a bit. You're going through these devotions saying, "That's right; I'm going to tell the devil a thing or two. He's going to get off my case today. That's right, Prophetess, I'm going to pray and release some authority. I'm going to stop being a wimp." Well, that's really good, and I sure don't mean to disappoint you, but let me just ask you a question: Does the Lord have full authority over you? Now, you really need to answer that question truthfully and honestly for yourself. This is a book! Nobody can see if your hand is raised or not.

The person God has authority over has the right to pray with authority. If He does not have authority over you, then you stay yourself on the asking ground because you don't have a right to be commanding. When one respects an authority figure, they obey that person's command.

When the Lord commands you to do something, do you offer some grand excuse? Are you one of those people who always has something to say, but rarely anything to do for Him? When He asks you to pray, do you obey or say:

"I can't pray right now; I'm too tired. Don't You know what time I put the children to bed? I'm just so exhausted. I don't have anymore energy. I can't get up at 5 o'clock to pray and still go to work. That's just too much. I'm already worn out." And so on and so on and so on . . .

Though it is true that the Lord has given you power and authority, have you really received it? Intellectually, you may have decided to receive the empowerment of praying with authority, but if God has no authority over you, then you don't have authority over the demons you're commanding because those demons have authority over you. You're either obeying the voice of the Lord, or you're not. No matter what half-stepping way you may try to justify it, you cannot serve two masters.

> *No man can serve two masters: for either he will hate the one, and love the other; or else he will hold to the one, and despise the other. Ye cannot serve God and mammon. Matthew 6:24*

God desires to have full authority over you in order for you to have full authority over the enemy. Submit yourself to the Lord this morning. Ask Him to create in you a clean heart and renew a right spirit within you. Ask Him to show you the error of your ways so that you can line up your life to His will

today. Ask Him to help you to be sensitive and attentive to His voice, and the next time He calls you, obey His authority and say, "Here I am, Lord."

Morning Glory

PRESSING IN

Have you felt like God has been pressing you out lately? It's not really a tangible feeling, but you can sense that your spirit is going through a change. God is pressing you to go higher and deeper, but you don't even want to think about that right now. You figure, "I'm deep enough now, Lord. I'm already fasting and praying. My goodness, how much deeper do I have to get? After awhile, I'm not going to have any life left. Why do I have to be so consumed? It's just Jesus in the morning; Jesus in the evening; Jesus, Jesus, Jesus, everywhere I go. Can't I just be a regular human being and do some normal activities sometimes?" Well, you are not alone. We are all being pressed out to work in the kingdom of God.

Press your way into the Lord's presence even though you may be facing opposition. When you haven't consecrated, the trials, temptations and tests you undergo can often make you feel unworthy. Right then, you need to bring yourself to a maturity in the Lord, and praise Him anyhow. You mature when you bless God right in the midst of your trials. Though you may have been confronted on your job and your boss may have been unfair, learn how to press pass all of that. Begin to say, "God, I praise You anyway. I had a rough day, but I thank You. I had a bad day, but I glorify You. I give You the praise because regardless of the circumstance, You are still worthy."

The devil wants to control you by your feelings. He wants you to be too tired to bless the Lord. He wants to completely drain all of your energy so that you won't have the desire nor the strength to pray. If you bless the Lord by faith and praise Him anyway, the Lord will draw nigh unto your situation and work it out. But, if you keep your mouth shut, you're giving the devil the victory. Choose to bless God in spite of your situation.

Do you know that sometimes your breakthrough hinges on your praise? I know some of you think that as big as your problems are, a praise just isn't going to cut it, but God is saying, "Yes it will." When you don't think anything is happening, your breakthrough seems afar off, and you can't feel a thing, that's when God is working it out for you. He doesn't need your feelings to do it; He's doing it without your emotions and natural intellect. Yet, He still wants your praise.

If you want to grow in your prayer life, then understand that you don't learn how to pray by reading about it or by studying it—those are only instructional methods. You learn how to pray by praying. You can't press in with your mouth shut. You can't press in being cute. You've got to open up your mouth and be a participant. Your spirit is hungering and thirsting after the presence of the Lord. Come out of the outer court, and go into the inner court. Go beyond the inner court, and enter into the Holy of holies. Don't stop praying until you feel His anointing. Don't stop until you feel His quickening power. Don't stop until the Holy Ghost overtakes you.

Devotional

The Lord wants to press you into victory. He wants to press you to another level. If you want your strength renewed, praise and glorify the Lord this morning. He's been good to you. Get into His presence. There's victory in your praise. Press beyond your flesh, and press into the realm of the Spirit. Ask the Lord to take you into the Holy of holies. Ask Him to take you to the victory side, the peace side, the joy side, the humility side, and the sacrificing side. If you want to be more like Him, then enter into the Potter's house this morning. Let Him crush your flesh so that He can mold you again. Bask in His presence and in the power of His anointing. Ask Him to help you to endure hardship, overcome, and stand against warfare like a good soldier. You need His help to have a steadfast mind and to stop wavering in your spirit, thoughts, speech, actions, and deeds. Be unmovable, always abounding in the work of the Lord.

I press toward the mark for the prize of the high calling of God in Christ Jesus. Philip. 3:14

Don't fall short of the goal today. Press in!

Morning Glory

PURGE & PURIFY

And he shall sit as a refiner and purifier of silver: and he shall purify the sons of Levi, and purge them as gold and silver, that they may offer unto the LORD an offering in righteousness. Malachi 3:3

Nothing in this devotional is going to work for you the way that it should until your life gets cleaned up. You've got to be clean! I'm after every chief that doesn't look like God, sound like God, or operate like God. If that's not what you want, then you might as well put this book down right now, because it's either holiness or hell; there is no in-between.

I have homework for you this morning. Write down the words "purge and purify". Define those words, find out their origin, and look up the words related to "purge and purify". Make sure that you fully understand the definitions. After you look that up, go through the Bible and find a Scripture about someone that had to be purified or made just for a purpose. Find a person in the Bible that had to go through a process before they got the goods, because it's time to stop thinking that somebody is going to come and blow on you, and poof, there it is—you just fell into it.

For one solid week, examine your activities. Take notice of everything you watch, read, and talk about. Ask yourself if it's pure and purged? If it's not, then cut it off. When talking to friends—before they even get started on a tangent—ask them if the conversation is going to be clean. If not, then kindly tell them to change the subject.

Look, you cannot be a rank sinner for years and then only read your Bible every blue moon. If you partied everyday, then in order for God to get that partying out of your flesh, you've got to purify everyday. Your level of purification has got to match the depth of sin that you came out of; otherwise, that sin will have the power to keep pulling you back into sinful things.

Without submitting to a process of purification, you'll forget that you've been purged from dead works. However, undergoing a daily purification process reminds you that you are not a sinner anymore; you're not a liar anymore; you don't drink anymore; you don't fornicate anymore.

We're not interested in being non-effective Christians. We should want to be purified to the bone. Anytime you're fighting purification, it's because your old nature wants to live again. You cannot grab a hold of God and still have your hands in the world at the same time. You've got to be purged.

Let me remind you: This book is not some sweet, neat, nice little treat where you just study some fluffy mess that has no impact on your life. This is a devotional and is intended to aid you in devoting yourself totally to God. It is for your spiritual enrichment. That means that I'm out to retrain and reconstruct your spirit man. Somewhere, your spirit got messed up and caused you to think and act like the world. Though you may not like this right now, get the junk out! You've got to be purged and purified.

The process of purification must be done regardless of your title; no one is excluded. You should never want to get so high and mighty that you're ashamed of going to the altar, nor should you desire to be so popular and renowned that you can't say, "Help me Lord." No call, office, or gift supercedes the purification process of the Lord.

God wants to get you ready to receive His blessings into your life, but you can't get them the way that you are right now. He wants to get you ready to operate with an anointing you've never had before and to be used in a realm you've never been used in before. You cannot afford to mess around. Begin to ask the Lord to get you ready. Ask Him to purge and purify you today. Make room for the Word of God in your belly. You may not understand it, but tell the Holy Ghost to get in your belly, and make room for His Word. Make room, make room, make room. It's too crowded; make room for the Lord. You're too full of yourself; make room. Too full of your own ideas; make room. Too full of your own pride; make room. Make room, in Jesus' name.

PUT ON YOUR ARMOR

Finally, my brethren, be strong in the Lord, and in the power of his might. Put on the whole armour of God, that ye may be able to stand against the wiles of the devil. Ephes. 6:10-11

"Put on." Does it say that God is going to do it for you or that someone else is going to strap you up? The reason you keep getting slapped down by the enemy is because you are not putting your armor on. How in the world are your pursing your two lips together talking about you're a mighty warrior for the Lord and you're not even suited up? What kind of soldier are you?

The Word says, "Put on the whole armor of God, that ye may be" what? "Able." When you're able, you're skilled and have enough power to operate skillfully. If you don't have your armor on, then you are unable to do to anything worth anything.

"Put on the whole armor of God, that ye may be able to" what? "Stand." When you're standing, you're in an upright position on your feet; you're rooted and grounded. You exude a certain confidence because you remain unchanged by circumstances, conditions, or opposition. You are stationary and stable. Now, if you're not standing, then just what do you think you are doing? Falling perhaps? Either you are standing or falling, going forward or going backwards, coming or going, believing or being deceived.

Okay, you put on your armor so that you may be able to stand how? "Against." When you assume the posture of standing against something, you are in direct contrast to it — a striking difference exists between you and that thing. When you're standing against something, you are prepared and you are ready; you're standing face to face with the enemy. By standing, you're not running from the enemy. Go ahead and take a stand against the enemy and declare:

"I'm not leaving my house; I'm going to stand. I'm not leaving my church; I'm going to stand. I'm not going to stand with the enemy; I'm standing against the enemy. Every time the devil throws a wile my way, I will stand against him."

If you are unable to stand, then there are things hitting your flesh and spirit that should be hitting your shield. Some issues are hitting your mind that should be hitting your helmet. When your feet are not shod with the preparation of the gospel of peace, you wander away from understanding.

"That hurt my feelings."

Where was your breastplate?

"I heard what they said about me."

Where was your helmet?

"I'm quitting the choir."

Where is your sword?

Put on the whole armor of God!

Stand therefore, having your loins girt about with truth, and having on the breastplate of righteousness; And your feet shod with the preparation of the gospel of peace; Above all, taking the shield of faith, wherewith ye shall be able to quench all the fiery darts of the wicked. And take the helmet of salvation, and the sword of the Spirit, which is the word of God: Praying always with all prayer and supplication in the Spirit, and watching thereunto with all perseverance and supplication for all saints; Ephes. 6:14-18

Morning Glory

Devotional

RECEIVING AN IMPARTATION

O h, today is your day; count on it. The Lord fashioned this day for you from the creation of time, for on this day, you shall receive an impartation. It is His desire to impart something directly into your life this morning.

Consider Hannah for a moment:

But unto Hannah he gave a worthy portion; for he loved Hannah: but the LORD had shut up her womb. And her adversary also provoked her sore, for to make her fret, because the LORD had shut up her womb. And as he did so year by year, when she went up to the house of the LORD, so she provoked her; therefore she wept, and did not eat. 1 Samuel 1:5-7

The first thing Hannah did to facilitate receiving an impartation from the Lord was to abstain from eating. The Lord used the enemy and adversary of her life to provoke her into a fast. Now understand something: You don't get an impartation from fasting; you fast to prepare for the impartation. Fasting kills every ungodly thing within you in order to prepare your spirit to receive from the Lord.

And she was in bitterness of soul, and prayed unto the LORD, and wept sore. And she vowed a vow, and said, O LORD of hosts, if thou wilt indeed look on the affliction of thine handmaid, and remember me, and not forget thine handmaid, but wilt give unto thine handmaid a man child, then I will give him unto the LORD all the days of his life, and there shall no razor come upon his head. 1 Samuel 1:10-11

Though Hannah was weeping and waxed bitter in her soul, she vowed a vow unto the Lord. In the midst of her pain, she was able to say, "God, if you give to me, then I'll give back to You." You need to know today that the words that come out of your mouth will release your victory. Though you may want things from the Lord, He's got to be able to know that if He gives it to you, will He get the glory, or will you hog it all up for yourself? You can't just constantly tell the Lord, "Give me this, give me that, gimme, gimme, gimme." What are you promising Him? If the Lord blesses you with a car, will you pick up the saints or just cruise by them while they're waiting at the bus stop?

And it came to pass, as she continued praying before the LORD, that Eli marked her mouth. Now Hannah, she spake in her heart; only her lips moved, but her voice was not heard: therefore Eli thought she had been drunken. And Eli said unto her, How long wilt thou be drunken? put away thy wine from thee. And Hannah answered and said, No, my lord, I am a woman of a sorrowful spirit: I have drunken neither wine nor strong drink, but have poured out my soul before the LORD. 1 Samuel 1:12-15

Hannah poured out her soul to the Lord. She began to rid herself of everything within her that was unlike God. You

see, before God can completely step in, there's got to be a cleansing out. There has to be a time when you finally realize that enough is enough. You've been trying to work it out your way and evidently that's not working.

For whatsoever is born of God overcometh the world: and this is the victory that overcometh the world, even our faith. 1 John 5:4

That which is from God is born with power to overcome. God's impartation jumps into you with the power to take you through. You don't need to back up from a fight with the enemy, because that which is from God has the power to stand against all of the wiles of the devil. The power I'm referring to doesn't shake, rattle, or roll. The power of the Lord is fortified.

But the manifestation of the Spirit is given to every man to profit withal. For to one is given by the Spirit the word of wisdom; to another the word of knowledge by the same Spirit; To another faith by the same Spirit; to another the gifts of healing by the same Spirit; To another the working of miracles; to another prophecy; to another discerning of spirits; to another divers kinds of tongues; to another the interpretation of tongues: 1 Cor. 12:7-10

During this season in your life, you need an impartation. You need one of the nine gifts of the Spirit for what you're going through. Well guess what? Receive it. Whatever gift you need to operate in, receive it today. Do you need faith? Receive it. Do you need knowledge? Receive it. Do you need wisdom? Receive it. Is it an interpretation anointing you need? Receive it. Are you in need of discernment? Receive it. Whatever it is that you need, glory be to God, receive it. You're on schedule today. You have been given an impartation. Receive it!

You may be in a situation right now that you don't know how to get out of. Well, the Lord is saying, "You've received the gift of wisdom. Operate therein." Does it seem as though you're in a no win situation? Receive the gift of miracles. Is somebody in your family sick? The Lord is saying, "Receive the impartation for the gift of healing. Receive it now." Oh come on; it's there for you this morning. Whatever you need, receive it today.

The Lord has imparted unto you today. Begin to thank Him by faith. If you'll only believe that you have received it, you shall have it. Believe that you have received it, and you shall have it. Believe that you have received it, and you shall have it. Believe that you have received it, and you shall have it. The Lord just keeps saying to you, "Believe that you have received it, and you shall have it. Believe that you have received it, and you shall have it!"

You may still be doubting, but I want to tell you that the Lord brought you to these pages in spite of your circumstances; He gave you an impartation. All you need to do is believe that you have received it. He didn't judge you and say that you weren't clean enough to receive it; He just said that you must believe.

Therefore I say unto you, What things soever ye desire, when ye pray, believe that ye receive them, and ye shall have them. Mark 11:24

All things are possible for you if you'll only believe.

And Jesus looking upon them saith, With men it is impossible, but not with God: for with God all things are possible. Mark 10:27

Morning Glory

RECEIVING THE REVELATION

All things are delivered unto me of my Father: and no man knoweth the Son, but the Father; neither knoweth any man the Father, save the Son, and he to whomsoever the Son will reveal him. Matthew 11:27

Do you know that it is impossible to have a natural understanding of the power of God unless it is revealed to you? To know Jesus is a revelation. The fact of the matter is that God doesn't reveal Himself to everyone. Why is it that out of all the people in your city and your family, something quickened your mortal mind, opened up your understanding, and caused you to believe that Jesus Christ was the Son of the living God? Anyone can easily pick up the Bible and start reading Scriptures. With all of the Gideon Bibles in hotels and motels throughout the world, many people have the opportunity to read God's Word; yet, the Holy Ghost urges those whom He chooses.

Why are you reading this book today? Nobody put a gun to your head, but you know what? There is something that God has for your life, and in order for Him to get you there, you've got to understand that the Lord and His Word must be revealed to you. You're not reading these pages by happenstance. God wants to give you a revelation of Who He is. He doesn't want to toy with your emotions and just have you jumping and shouting. He wants to be revealed to you in a greater measure this morning. He wants you to know His ins and outs. He wants you to know His character so that when you're faced with something, you'll come before His presence knowing His will.

Everyone goes through their own "Simon Peter" season; it's your turn now. Jesus' had twelve disciples and a throng of followers; yet, out of everyone around them, Simon Peter received the revelation. That means that revelation knowledge doesn't occur to everyone. Just because there's a thousand people in a church does not necessarily mean that a thousand people are receiving God's revelation.

He saith unto them, But whom say ye that I am? And Simon Peter answered and said, Thou art the Christ, the Son of the living God. And Jesus answered and said unto him, Blessed art thou, Simon Barjona: for flesh and blood hath not revealed it unto thee, but my Father which is in heaven. And I say also unto thee, That thou art Peter, and upon this rock I will build my church; and the gates of hell shall not prevail against it. Matthew 16:15-18

Even if you feel like you're in the basement of life today, God still wants to reveal Himself to you; after all, He is the Lily of the Valley. You are reading this today because the Lord wants you to know that you're about to be a foundation He can build and establish Himself upon. The gates of hell shall not prevail against you.

Devotional

No weapon that is formed against thee shall prosper; and every tongue that shall rise against thee in judgment thou shalt condemn. This is the heritage of the servants of the LORD, and their righteousness is of me, saith the LORD. Isaiah 54:17

The anointing is on you this day . . . it's on you right now. The Lord is opening up your mind to the revelation of Who He is. You may have awakened this morning feeling heavy, but God is lifting the burden from you today. The revelation you've just received is being illuminated throughout your life and NOTHING—no thing—shall prevail against it!

Meditate on the fact that you are unmovable, unshakable, and unwavering this morning. Meditate on the fact that no matter what comes your way, it did not, can not, and will not prevail against you. Thank the Lord for molding you into a solid rock today. Thank Him because out of everyone in the world, He knew you and still chose to reveal Himself to you. The Lord has been good to you. Receive His revelation this morning. Allow that revelation to rejuvenate, renew, and refresh you today.

Wherefore gird up the loins of your mind, be sober, and hope to the end for the grace that is to be brought unto you at the revelation of Jesus Christ; 1 Peter 1:13

RENEWING THE SPIRIT OF YOUR MIND

Some of you are bound up in your mind, but God wants to free you today. You're in a battle for the rest of your life, and it's high time that you start acting like it. You're going to stop living your life defeated. Stop walking crazy, looking crazy, and talking crazy.

What are you going to do?

"I don't know."

Where are you going to go?

"I don't know."

What are you going to do in life?

"I don't know."

Do you want to go to school?

"I don't know."

Where do you want to work?

"I don't know. Whatever the Lord says."

Stop saying "I don't know"; that's just a cop-out. The Bible tells you that you shall have whatsoever you say, and saying "I don't know" about everything is not saying anything!

Have you ever seen people waiting on the Lord, and that's it? Nevermind the fact that they're getting put out of their house; they're just waiting on the Lord. What happened to the Bible saying:

But thou shalt remember the LORD thy God: for it is he that giveth thee power to get wealth, that he may establish his covenant which he sware unto thy fathers, as it is this day. Deut. 8:18

If they know that they've been given the power to get wealth, then what do you think hinders them from getting it? Their mind.

And be not conformed to this world: but be ye transformed by the renewing of your mind, that ye may prove what is that good, and acceptable, and perfect, will of God. Romans 12:2

The spirit of your mind has to be renewed. I wish I could just whisper that into your ear right now. You don't have to wallow in defeat. When the Spirit quickened within you, you were quickened to life more abundantly. You used to be dead in your sins, but God gave you life abundantly. You are not the same person. Do you realize that? You simply are not the same.

Where is the victory in your life? You may have stopped drinking, smoking, cursing, and fornicating, but is your mind still trapped? You love the Lord, but where's your joy? You may have stripped yourself from sin, but did you put on the garment of praise.

To appoint unto them that mourn in Zion, to give unto them beauty for ashes, the oil of joy for mourning, the garment of praise for the spirit of heaviness; that they might be called trees of righteousness, the planting of the LORD, that he might be glorified. Isaiah 61:3

And be renewed in the spirit of your mind; Ephes. 4:23

Let this mind be in you, which was also in Christ Jesus: Philip. 2:5

Renew your mind this morning by forgetting your past and those things that hinder you from soaring in the Spirit. Renew your mind by being consistent in the things of God. Renew your mind by concentrating on the Lord. Stay focused and remember that renewing your mind is not just something to do this morning as a devotion. Totally devote yourself to a constant renewal process of your mind. How?

Finally, brethren, whatsoever things are true, whatsoever things are honest, whatsoever things are just, whatsoever things are pure, whatsoever things are lovely, whatsoever things are of good report; if there be any virtue, and if there be any praise, think on these things. Philip. 4:8

Morning Glory

STANDING ON THE WORD OF GOD

It is the spirit that quickeneth; the flesh profiteth nothing: the words that I speak unto you, they are spirit, and they are life. John 6:63

Our walk with God is judged according to our Word level. We feel the anointing and think that feeling is what makes us deep; not so. The amount of Word in your belly is what gives you depth. How much have you eaten lately?

In order for the Spirit of God to operate in you, it has to stand on a foundation. If there's no foundation in you, then you'll wander in and out of the realm of familiar spirits. That means that you'll do things that look like God and sound like God, but, actually, is not God. You could be speaking in tongues, praying, singing and dancing, but still be operating under a spirit of deception.

A whole host of people love the spiritual and are sincerely in love with the anointing; however, you'll rarely find someone that's just as in love with the commitment that comes along with the anointing. The devil could care less how many tears you shed. The only thing that backs the devil up is the Word of God that comes out of your belly—not the

Word that you've read, but the Word that you genuinely believe. You can read 199 Scriptures and not believe a single word; therefore, it will not work for you.

The Word of God is infallible and was never designed to work in the carnal realm; it was designed to operate where the anointing is. You cannot live in carnality and all of a sudden when you want something or it's convenient for you, try to manipulate the Word into working for you in your foul, carnal state. In order for the Word to operate in your life, it has to be encompassed around the Spirit of God.

If God ever gave His Word to you, then it doesn't matter how bleak a situation looks, wait until your change comes. Know that He's on the way because He gave you His Word.

"Did you see anything?"

"No, but I have His Word."

"Can you feel anything?"

"No, but I have His Word, and I don't have to feel it because I know that I have it. I'm standing on the infallible, unchanging Word of the Lord. He gave me a promise and His Word says that He is faithful to perform it. He promised to never leave me or forsake me. I may not see Him, but I know He's here; His Word says that He is with me always."

If you want to be anointed in a greater measure, then sit down and study your Bible because when the Lord's anointing descends, it's coming in search of His Word.

"I want to lay hands on the sick."

Is that in your belly? Is the Scripture for healing truly

lodged within your spirit? Do you really believe it?

"I want to cast out devils."

Has your spiritual mind understood that God has given you authority to cast out devils? Under who's authority are you to cast out demons? You've got to know what you can do. Once you've read how to cast out demons, how to lay hands on the sick, how to be an overcomer, how to have more joy, and how to have more peace, then when the Lord is looking for somebody to use, He'll find the person that understands and believes His Word.

Never belittle the Word of the Lord. The Spirit cannot get around you without getting the Word of God. The Word is the action force for the Spirit of God. It is the steering wheel that keeps you from driving off of the highway.

Now, be mindful of how you go about getting the Word of God.

"I know this is the one. It's been confirmed. The Lord Himself showed this to me. I wasn't even thinking about and it, and whew, my Bible just fell over to this Scripture."

I know that may seem funny, but there are many saints who go about reading their Bibles just like that. Wherever it falls, they think that's what the Lord wants them read. No, Lucky Strike! This isn't the lottery!

Commune with the Lord before you open up His Word. While you're communing, be sensitive to the voice of the Spirit. If He says, "Peace", then get your Bible and read everything that has to do with peace. Don't just sit there with your Bible in front of an open window and wait for the wind to blow it to a certain page. Study to show yourself approved.

Study to shew thyself approved unto God, a workman that needeth not to be ashamed, rightly dividing the word of truth. 2 Tim. 2:15

Thank the Lord this morning for His Word. Thank Him for the revelation of His Word coming alive right now in your spirit and in your mind. Claim the results and walk therein. Thank Him because you're going to accomplish the things that He's set in your spirit to do through the acknowledgment and understanding of His Word.

Devotional

STIR UP THE GIFT WITHIN YOU

But the manifestation of the Spirit is given to every man to profit withal. For to one is given by the Spirit the word of wisdom; to another the word of knowledge by the same Spirit; To another faith by the same Spirit; to another the gifts of healing by the same Spirit; To another the working of miracles; to another prophecy; to another discerning of spirits; to another divers kinds of tongues; to another the interpretation of tongues: 1 Cor. 12:7-10

Those are the nine gifts of the Holy Spirit. The number "nine" usually represents giving birth. That means that those nine gifts have to be in your belly. Once you get filled with the Holy Ghost, those nine gifts must mature within you. Just as a woman conceives in her belly, you've got to carry God's gifts full-term before they can be used. When conception occurs in the natural, one doesn't get pregnant today and then deliver a baby tomorrow. Likewise, there's also a maturation process in the spiritual realm before one can deliver the nine gifts of the Spirit.

If you've been filled with the Holy Ghost, then in you, right now, are all nine gifts. Saying you have the Holy

Ghost without the nine gifts is just like saying you have Jesus in you but not God. When you have the Holy Ghost, the gifts come with Him. Where are they? Stuck behind your fleshly, unconsecrated mind.

I beseech you therefore, brethren, by the mercies of God, that ye present your bodies a living sacrifice, holy, acceptable unto God, which is your reasonable service. And be not conformed to this world: but be ye transformed by the renewing of your mind, that ye may prove what is that good, and acceptable, and perfect, will of God. Romans 12:1-2

When you cease to live according to the appetites of your flesh and start living in obedience to the will of God, then the gifts of the Spirit will begin to manifest itself with power in your life. Your being has to be controlled by the Word of God within in you.

Your only way of proving that God is alive in you is by using the Word to transform your mind. That's a 24-hour job which means you will not have time to be concentrating on what other people are doing. You won't have time to be listening to foolishness. Renew your mind, or every time you fast, pray, and study the Word of God, something will come to choke the Word out.

The gifts of the Spirit are bigger than any devil you will ever face. It's bigger than your situation, your circumstance, and your mind because it is a spiritual gift. It never stops working. It's working while you're sleeping. It's also doing battle for you when you can't even see the enemy.

Whatever you need this morning, put your gift in operation. The gift of God within you is getting ready to work out your situation. It fights for you, works out your problem, eases your mind, and heals your emotions. Stir it up everyday. Don't leave the house until you stir it up. Right there in your room, start praising God until you stir up that gift. Keep on blessing the Lord until you feel it. If you've got to stand there for thirty minutes, stay until you feel the gift awaken within you.

When you go out today, use your gift. While you're driving, use your gift. When you wake up, use it. Use it in the kitchen; use it while you're washing clothes; use it while you're combing your hair; use it while you're in the shower. Use it. Stop saving it for church services—it's not a church gift; it's a spiritual gift. The gifts of the Spirit transcend doors and walls and flesh. You don't have to contain it; just use it. Don't hold the gift hostage; use it. Whatever you need today, stir up one of the gifts of the Spirit. Stir up the gift within you.

STRENGTH

For thou hast girded me with strength to battle: them that rose up against me hast thou subdued under me. 2 Samuel 22:40

You are a powerful threat to the kingdom of darkness. Believe me, the enemy knows all about you. He has to know who you are in order to know who he's fighting. He wouldn't be after you if he didn't think you're a force to be reckoned with. He's not playing games with you and just wasting his time. Do you know that he wouldn't try to stop you if God hadn't already given you the green light to go? You're not some mere underling. If the enemy comes after you, then you must be some big cheese! The funny thing is that the devil knows some things about you that you don't even know about yourself. That's why he tries to stop you before you really come into the full knowledge of all that God has called you to be.

Many Christians often forfeit doing great things in the Lord because they are comfortable remaining crybabies and resist maturing in the things of Christ. Instead, they persist in sulking about people talking about them or lying on them. Instead of gaining strength, they live in constant fear of being backstabbed or hurt, and, therefore, concede their victory to their enemy (the devil). Never for a moment do they stop to consider that God may be trying to work some strength in them.

Decide now that no matter what the opposition, trial or test, you will stand up and be strong. The Lord is gracing you with strength this morning. Don't be scared of it. Embrace it. You're stronger than you can even fathom because the power of Almighty God lives within you. Grab a hold to God's strength. It's not by YOUR might or power, but by His Spirit. Lean on Him for your strength today. Come on, you can make it. You can go through whatever is confronting you. The Lord is equipping you today with strength. You are His anointed and chosen one, so stay strong. Even in your weakness, the Lord will be made strong.

The LORD is my strength and my shield; my heart trusted in him, and I am helped: therefore my heart greatly rejoiceth; and with my song will I praise him. The LORD is their strength, and he is the saving strength of his anointed. Psalm 28:7-8

Morning Glory

TESTIMONY POWER

By faith Enoch was translated that he should not see death; and was not found, because God had translated him: for before his translation he had this testimony, that he pleased God. Hebrews 11:5

When you have taken a death walk, you are able to talk about the things you've died to. If you died to it, then those things are buried and are no longer a part of you; therefore, there should be no semblance of it in your life. It's a secret unless you chose to tell it. Testifying resurrects the memory of what God has done for you. Because you have been justified, there should be no telltale signs of what you used to be, and therein lies the power of your testimony. In essence, if you've been delivered from alcohol and nicotine, then you should no longer look like you're still drinking and smoking.

There are many people struggling with the same problems that once ailed you. They have no hope and cannot see their way out. They don't have the faith to believe that they'll make it through the next day, let alone have enough faith to believe in what they cannot see. Your testimony is viable proof and evidence of the grace, mercy, and love of the Lord. When you tell someone about your death walk, they are able to see the tangible power of God in full operation. It is then that you become a living testimony.

And they overcame him by the blood of the Lamb, and by the word of their testimony; and they loved not their lives unto the death. Rev. 12:11

Your testimony makes you an overcomer. You don't have to be ashamed of your past—you overcame it. When you overcame it, you conquered it. When you took the death walk, you separated yourself from the stench of your past.

Sharing your testimony expresses your gratitude to God for freeing you from a life of sin and death. Now that you are free, the power of your testimony resoundingly declares that nothing shall separate you from the love of Christ Jesus, our Lord. Therefore, not only are you an overcomer, but you are also more than a conqueror.

Who shall separate us from the love of Christ? shall tribulation, or distress, or persecution, or famine, or nakedness, or peril, or sword? As it is written, For thy sake we are killed all the day long; we are accounted as sheep for the slaughter. Nay, in all these things we are more than conquerors through him that loved us. For I am persuaded, that neither death, nor life, nor angels, nor principalities, nor powers, nor things present, nor things to come, Nor height, nor depth, nor any other creature, shall be able to separate us from the love of God, which is in Christ Jesus our Lord. Romans 8:35-39

Remember: The Lord didn't save you just for yourself. He saved you so that after you became converted, you can be a living witness and shining example to someone else so that they can also come out of the bondage of sin and death. Go

back and get someone else today so that they too can be strengthened.

> *But I have prayed for thee, that thy faith fail not: and when thou art converted, strengthen thy brethren. Luke 22:32*

When you share the power of your testimony, you transform a sinner's mind. Now they are able to see God is real, where once they had been blind.

To them, the Lord is no longer a fairytale, myth, or fable, Because your testimony powerfully proved that your God is indeed well able.

> *Wherefore he is able also to save them to the uttermost that come unto God by him, seeing he ever liveth to make intercession for them. Hebrews 7:25*

> *Now unto him that is able to do exceeding abundantly above all that we ask or think, according to the power that worketh in us, Ephes. 3:20*

TRUSTING THE ALPHA AND OMEGA

For whom he did foreknow, he also did predestinate to be conformed to the image of his Son, that he might be the firstborn among many brethren. Romans 8:29

Before you ever asked the Lord to come into your life, He already knew you. He chose you before the foundation of the world. You were saved through His grace and mercy. When you were in the disco, the Lord marked you as His own. With the crack-pipe in your mouth, He knew you would belong to Him. While you were losing your virginity, He put His claim on you. You were destined to be in the Lord. Before you even repented, He already had it figured out. He knew you from the beginning, and you can be sure that He also knows the end.

Not everyone has a destiny in the Lord, but you do. How blessed you are to be found within His will! Do you know that you are right on schedule? The things that are surfacing in your life are all on schedule. You need to look at your situation and learn the lessons. For instance, if God is getting ready to teach you a lesson about lying, He will schedule a lie to surface out of you. You then will know that you've still got a lying spirit and then be able to rebuke it out of your life. There's no need to worry; it's all on schedule. The Lord is not through with you yet, for His Word says:

Moreover whom he did predestinate, them he also called: and whom he called, them he also justified: and whom he justified, them he also glorified. Romans 8:30

You are still being justified in order that you might ultimately be glorified. Trust that God is Who He says He is. He is able to see down the road and knows each path you should take. He sees beyond the obstacles; therefore, lean not on your own understanding, but lean on Him. Before you even call on the Lord, He's answering you because He already knows your end.

And it shall come to pass, that before they call, I will answer; and while they are yet speaking, I will hear. Isaiah 65:24

Whatever issue is sitting on the table of your heart today, God knows the outcome. He'll start you on a new beginning, but you've got to trust Him to get you to the end. Call on the Alpha and Omega this morning. The Lord is your Beginning, and He is your End.

I am Alpha and Omega, the beginning and the ending, saith the Lord, which is, and which was, and which is to come, the Almighty.

Rev. 1:8

UNCOVERING THE MYSTERIES OF GOD

In that hour Jesus rejoiced in spirit, and said, I thank thee, O Father, Lord of heaven and earth, that thou hast hid these things from the wise and prudent, and hast revealed them unto babes: even so, Father; for so it seemed good in thy sight. Luke 10:21

You don't have to be a Prophet, Evangelist, Apostle, Pastor, or Teacher to understand the mystery of God's Word. There are some mysteries in the Bible that have not been revealed to men of intellect, but God has chosen to reveal them to babes in Christ because of their innocence. Though you may not be in the five-fold ministry, never feel excluded from receiving revelation knowledge from the Lord. In fact, you ought to thank God that you're ready for the unveiling of His mystery. Because of innocence, hunger, and thirst, God will reveal some things to you "that eyes have not seen, and ears have not heard." Hallelujah!

Perhaps one of the greatest mysteries of God is when He takes people who may not measure up to the world's standard, transforms them, and then uses them mightily for His work. When you're saying, "I can't do it; I don't know how I'm going to make it," know that you're ripe for a mystery in

God to be revealed. Perhaps your mind can't understand how God can take a drug addicted, chain-smoking, lying cheater, clean that person up, and put His Word in his belly. That's a mystery revealed.

Unless God reveals Himself, you'd never see Him. When the Lord opens up another level of understanding for you, realize that you've just been given a gift from God. Haven't you ever read a particular Scripture over, and over, and over again, and it only meant one thing to you? All of a sudden, right in the midst of your trial, you read those same verses again, and your victory seemingly jumps off of the page. At that moment, God granted you favor and revealed Himself to you.

> *In whom we have redemption through his blood, the forgiveness of sins, according to the riches of his grace; Wherein he hath abounded toward us in all wisdom and prudence; Having made known unto us the mystery of his will, according to his good pleasure which he hath purposed in himself: Ephes. 1:7-9*

If there are some things happening in your life that you just don't understand, then there are some mysteries that you need to discover this morning. Receive the revelation God wants to reveal to you. Ask Him to open your eyes, ears, heart and mind to receive afresh from Him. Let Him feed you a rhema Word today. The Lord will enlighten the eyes of your under-standing this morning . . . uncover the mysteries of God.

*That the God of our Lord Jesus Christ, the Father of glory, may give
unto you the spirit of wisdom and revelation in the knowledge of him:
The eyes of your understanding being enlightened; that ye may know
what is the hope of his calling, and what the riches of the glory of his
inheritance in the saints, Ephes. 1:17-18*

Morning Glory

UNDER-STANDING UNDERSTANDING

Make me to understand the way of thy precepts: so shall I talk of thy wondrous works. Psalm 119:27

Do you know that you can go through a whole bunch of trials and tribulations with the Lord, and still lack understanding? I remember when the Lord told me that I didn't understand Him. I said, "Yes I do, Lord. I understand that You delivered me from drugs. I understand that when I had a nervous breakdown, You restored my mind. I understand that You were there for me when my marriage didn't work out, I didn't have any money, and I was on welfare. Lord, I do understand. After all that we've been through together, why are You telling me that I don't understand?"

Right then, the Lord directed me to the dictionary. No, I didn't need to go to a theologian that time, just Webster's. I looked up the word "under". It means something that is concealed and beneath the surface. Then, I looked up the word "stand". Stand means to be unchangeable and unmovable, regardless of circumstance; it means that against everything, you're still standing.

Wherefore take unto you the whole armour of God, that ye may be able to withstand in the evil day, and having done all, to stand. Stand therefore, having your loins girt about with truth, and having on the breastplate of righteousness; Ephes. 6:13-14

Having done all to stand, stand.

The reason some of you can't stand is because you're always running to somebody to rescue you from being under. When your back is against the wall and a bill is overdue, you run to your favorite family member to ask for a loan so that you can get from under that bill. Don't you understand that God put you under there so that you'd be able to stand? If you can't get through a light bill, how can He give you a mortgage? If you hyperventilate over your grocery bill, then how can the Lord give you a car note? Sometimes when you're crying out for help, the Lord is telling you, "No. You're not getting any help; go through this. I'm trying to get you to understand that I am the door. I'm your true source. I am Who you need."

Wisdom is the principal thing; therefore get wisdom: and with all thy getting get understanding. Proverbs 4:7

Understand this: You are not reading this by mistake. You're reading this today because you've been under something. The Lord wants you to know that when you come under depression and oppression, gossip, lies, ridicule, and pressure, He's gracing you to be under, because it's only the under that gives you the power to stand. That power belongs

Devotional

to you this morning. If you're ready to get out from being under, then you've got to trust the Lord, and determine that no matter how a situation looks, you are going to stand.

Happy is the man that findeth wisdom, and the man that getteth understanding. Proverbs 3:13

USING THE SWORD OF THE SPIRIT

Have you ever wondered why the devil hates you? He's like a disgruntled ex-employee. God created you with windpipes in your chest, and every time the devil's hears you praising God, it brings excruciating pain to his ears. He remembers that somebody else now has the job he once had. Whenever you quote the Bible, he hears God's voice, and he cannot stand it.

And God said, Let us make man in our image, after our likeness: and let them have dominion over the fish of the sea, and over the fowl of the air, and over the cattle, and over all the earth, and over every creeping thing that creepeth upon the earth. Genesis 1:26

You are made in the Lord's image and have dominion over all of the earth and every moving thing. Satan was cast down from heaven to the earth; therefore, since you have dominion over the earth, every time he makes a move, you have the power to dominate him and make him stop. You can tell the devil, "Halt. Take your hands off. Loosen your hold. Shut your mouth. Be still, in Jesus' name." Even in your weakest state, you still have power over the enemy.

Ye are of God, little children, and have overcome them: because greater is he that is in you, than he that is in the world. 1 John 4:4

Behold, I give unto you power to tread on serpents and scorpions, and over all the power of the enemy: and nothing shall by any means hurt you. Luke 10:19

Do you realize who you are? You are the greater one. You are the empowered overcomer. Every time you quote a Scripture, the devil runs and stops up his ears, because you have the power; that's right—YOU! You have authority over every thing beneath your feet—including planes, trains, and automobiles. Realize that the Spirit of God lives, dwells, and has It's being inside of you. Power! It's not just a word; it's an action. You've got to use it. The Lord packs you with power, then tells you to put on the whole armor of God so that you can protect that power from seeping out. Before you step out into warfare, take a look in the mirror and say, "I've got power. I've got my armor on with the helmet and the shield. Whatever the devil throws at me, I know that I am covered."

Now watch this: The Lord has also given you the most effective arsenal known to mankind. He said, "Now take the sword of the Spirit." Not only will you be able to stand against the wiles of the enemy, but every now and then, you even get to throw in a lick yourself. I'm talking about power!

Are you ready for your remedy for whatever hits you today. Your strategy is in His Word. Some people just love Bible study, but they need to go further than just reading

God's Word. Using the Word of God has got to become a way of life. Allow the Word of God to permeate your spirit so that you can stand against opposition and not crumble when problems arise.

Do you know at least 3 Scriptures? I double dare you to quote the three that you know. If you don't know any Scriptures, then for the next 60 seconds, go to your Bible and find three, powerful Scriptures. At the top of your lungs, start quoting those Scriptures and watch the anointing rise within you. You see, sometimes shouting "Hallelujah" isn't enough—you've got to have some Word springing up from your inner man. Open up your mouth and speak the Word of God into your life this morning.

Have you chosen your three Scriptures yet? Okay, each time you get one Scripture, read it aloud, and then praise the Lord. That means you'll read the 1st Scripture aloud. Stop. Praise. Then, read the 2nd Scripture aloud. Stop. Praise. And finally, do the same thing for the 3rd Scripture–read it aloud. Stop. Praise. Each time you do this, God is going to take you to another level in Him.

Today, you're going to walk out with some substance. If something is bothering you, counter it with His Word this morning. Your victory is in the Word. Your anointing is in the Word. Your life is in the Word.

Every demon spirit that's been holding you captive must flee this morning. Every tormenting devil is served notice to vacate. Lay your hands on your stomach and seal the Word of God in your belly. The devil must let go. He must get out of your mind. Allow the power of God's Word to chase him out of your mind and spirit.

This morning, after you get through reading, God is going to develop in you a new appetite for His Word. Taste and see that the Lord is good today. Read His Word with authority. The devil needs to hear you read it. It's not just coming out of your mouth; it's also going into your spirit. Victory is yours today. The Lord will destroy every yoke, and loosen every burden.

Okay, are you ready for your deliverance? Then pick up your Sword and slash the enemy. On guard!

Devotional

Morning Glory

VICTORY

There's nothing like slapping the devil back; that's what prayer is—slapping the devil back and knocking him out. Learn how to hit the devil in prayer. You are the winner. You are the overcomer. You are more than a conqueror. If you keep being passive, you'll never have any victories, peace or joy. The devil isn't tickling you, so don't just stand there moping around.

The Bible says:

And from the days of John the Baptist until now the kingdom of heaven suffereth violence, and the violent take it by force. Matthew 11:12

While reading this devotional, you've got to be a participant. This isn't just easy reading; it is to help make you free. You ought to be tired of the devil beating up on you. You are a child of the King of kings and the Lord of lords. Reclaim your rightful place and take back all that the devil has stolen from you. Take it by force!

When you don't think you have the victory, praise your way over into it. The devil wants you to keep your mouth shut. He doesn't want you to be able to say anything. He wants you to feel so dejected and rejected that you sink deeper and deeper into defeat. That's why you cannot rely on your feelings; the Word of God is not subject to how you feel.

Every aspect, nature, and personality of God operates in a spirit form. Joy is a spirit. Peace is a spirit. And, guess what? Victory is a spirit too.

The Lord has made it plain to us in His Word that you need supernatural faith in order to release victory. I'm not talking about the kind of faith where you believe God for houses and cars. What I'm talking about is if you have ever believed that the Lord raised Jesus from the dead and He now lives, then that's the faith you need for victory. That belief gives you victory in every area of your life. That's a powerful nugget right there.

> *But thanks be to God, which giveth us the victory through our Lord Jesus Christ. 1 Cor. 15:57*

> *For whatsoever is born of God overcometh the world: and this is the victory that overcometh the world, even our faith. 1 John 5:4*

> *He will swallow up death in victory; and the Lord GOD will wipe away tears from off all faces; and the rebuke of his people shall he take away from off all the earth: for the LORD hath spoken it.*
> *Isaiah 25:8*

Some people are fasting and praying and crying and weeping for the victory. Why? The victory is already yours; walk in it. Are you saved? Then, know that every time you open your eyes, you wake up into victory. That means anything you're going to face, you're going to have the

victory in it. It may not seem like you're victorious; nevertheless, the victory is already yours. In fact, begin to tell yourself
right now, "The victory is already mine."

Now, if God says that you have the victory, then that must
mean Satan does not have it. You should not be living a
defeated life. You don't need to say that you need victory; you
already have it. It was yours yesterday; it's yours today, and
it will be yours tomorrow.

Watch this:

> *So when this corruptible shall have put on incorruption, and this
> mortal shall have put on immortality, then shall be brought to pass
> the saying that is written, Death is swallowed up in victory. O death,
> where is thy sting? O grave, where is thy victory? 1 Cor. 15:54-55*

Even in death, you'll have victory! Death cannot sting you
because the Lord has already swallowed it up. You have life
eternal. That's powerful. Any situation that looks like it's
dried up, dead, and gone, speak life to that thing this
morning. God didn't leave any stones unturned. In every
circumstance, you have the victory and Satan is defeated.

Don't let the devil deceive you into accepting defeat. If you
think that you're defeated, you're not operating in the right
spirit; you're still operating by the mandates of this world and
by what your flesh is dictating. That's why we have to crucify
the old nature in order that we can walk in the victory that
God has already won for us.

Are you sick of walking in defeat, sick of lack, and sick of the devil in your home? The devil has been trying to rob you of your blessing. He'll even have you believing you're not saved if you let him. He craves for you to quit and wallow in defeat, but God said that the devil is a liar. The Lord has drawn you right to this page today because He is anointing you. The Lord is restoring you to your proper place and giving you the power to fight today.

This morning, rebuke the devil with your praise. Every time you shout "Hallelujah", you are celebrating the Lord and, thereby, condemning the devil. When you proclaim, "Glory," you're casting the enemy out of your life. When you say, "Lord, I thank You," you're embracing the anointing, and you're canceling the devil's contract. Come on and bless the Lord this morning. You've got to want the anointing, the victory, and the power.

Are you ready to participate in your victory? Ask the Lord to break your flesh in His presence. Kill the flesh before the flesh kills you. Ask him to break your will. Ask Him to break the old you, and create in you a new heart. Don't run from the test; don't run from the trial, for greater is He that is in you than he that is in the world. If you'll just open up your mouth and praise the Lord, victory will be yours today. Come on and do it. You've participated in your defeat long enough. Now, participate in your victory.

"Father, we praise You for making us more than a conqueror. We praise You for making us a victor. We praise You for making us an overcomer. Thank You for making us

Devotional

above and not beneath. Thank You for making us the head
and not the tail. In the matchless name of Jesus, we claim our
full inheritance. Today, we take back what the devil has stolen
from us. We take it back with authority. We take it by force
with the Word in the name of Jesus, and we claim victory
now. We claim deliverance now. We claim peace and joy now.
We claim overcoming power. We're leaning and depending on
You this morning to take us to another level. We release
victory into our minds, into our hearts, and into our everyday
lives. We want the devil to know when he sees us coming that
we have already conquered him through the blood of Jesus
Christ. We decree Your Word this morning. By the authority
of God, we shall live in the abundance of Christ, live under the
anointing, live in victory, live in faith, and live in revelation
knowledge. We shall rise above the storm, rise above the pain,
rise above the gossip, and rise above the lies. We shall overcome every fiery dart, overcome every tribulation, and
overcome every persecution. We're going to make it in the
kingdom, make it on our job, make it in our home, and make
it at our school because we are victorious. We've got the
victory because Your Word says that no weapon formed
against us shall prosper. Lord, we decree Your Word over our
lives today. We bind the very spirit and nature of poverty, and
we loose the spirit of wealth. We bind the spirit of persecution,
and we loose the spirit of praise. We bind the spirit of a broken
heart, and we loose the spirit of love. Thank You for winning
our victory, Lord. In Jesus' name. Amen."

Morning Glory

The Lord drew you to these pages this morning. He's communing with you and desires to impart directly into your life today. The Lord is saying to you:

"I'm transmitting today. I'm taking you up to another level; I'm graduating you today. I'm bringing you out of the dungeon; I'm bringing you out of the mess; I'm bringing you out of confusion; I'm establishing your heart; I'm establishing your spirit; I'm changing your mind; I'm fortifying you; I'm putting you in a steadfast place; I'm strengthening you. I want you to praise Me. Come on up. Begin to shout out of your spirit; begin to break out. You've been in bondage long enough. Break out. You've been defeated long enough. Break out as if you're breaking out of jail. Break out in the praise; break out in the shout. Come on. The devil needs to hear you shout; you need to hear yourself shout. You need to hear what your voice sounds like shouting in victory. Get familiar with the sound of victory in your own voice. You need to hear your voice praising Me. Open up your mouth; your ears need to hear you shout. Your ears need to hear you break out. Break out of that legalistic spirit. Break out of that religious and denominational spirit. Break into the Holy Spirit. I'm breaking every struggle; I'm breaking ever fetter; I'm taking you above it. Believe and trust in Me. I'm taking you above it, saith the Lord. Today, I'm taking you above weakness. I'm taking you above fear. You do have a sound mind. You do have the spirit of love. You do have the power today to rebuke the devil. You will not walk as a weak Christian after today, but you will walk in authority. I am your authority, and it is I who picks you up. I pick you up out of complacency, up out of mediocrity, up out of a broken heart. I take you up today. Come up out of the gutter, up out of depression, up out of discouragement, up out of despondency, up out of error, up out of mistakes, up out of weakness, up out of lust, up out of carnality, up out of your old nature, up out of your old desires. Up, up, up. Come up."

Thine, O LORD, is the greatness, and the power, and the glory, and the victory, and the majesty: for all that is in the heaven and in the earth is thine; thine is the kingdom, O LORD, and thou art exalted as head above all. 1 Chron. 29:11

VOWS

If a man vow a vow unto the LORD, or swear an oath to bind his soul with a bond; he shall not break his word, he shall do according to all that proceedeth out of his mouth. Numbers 30:2

Do you know that God remembers all of the vows you make to Him? You may think you were making a bunch of mumbo-jumbo promises to God at the altar, but you're responsible for your vows unto the Lord. Perhaps you may have said, "Lord, please just do this one thing for me and I promise I'll never do that again." Remember that?

When thou vowest a vow unto God, defer not to pay it; for he hath no pleasure in fools: pay that which thou hast vowed. Eccles. 5:4

Heed the Word of the God and don't be a fool. Live up to your words. They are powerful and expose the depth and character of your soul. Your word says it all.

When thou shalt vow a vow unto the LORD thy God, thou shalt not slack to pay it: for the LORD thy God will surely require it of thee; and it would be sin in thee. Deut. 23:21

You need to be credible and responsible for the covenants you enter into; that also includes your bills. When you signed the payment agreement for that credit card company, they

trusted your word. Don't make people regret the trust that they place in you. Honor the vows you make at church and to different ministries. Keep your word. Your word is your bond. Stop making promises you cannot keep, and make sure that your actions line up with your words.

Just as you put the Lord in remembrance of His Word and promises to you, this morning He wants to put you in remembrance of a few things you have promised Him. Rededicate yourself to the Lord in act, word, service, and deed. He deserves your most solemn pledge and promise.

Morning Glory

WAITING ON THE LORD

When you're standing on a promise from the Lord, waiting should not be burdensome. When He wakes you up in the midnight hour and speaks to your spirit, no devil in hell should be able to make you doubt what God is saying. You travailed and persevered for His Word. You lamented until He answered; now, stand on that Word and wait.

But they that wait upon the LORD shall renew their strength; they shall mount up with wings as eagles; they shall run, and not be weary; and they shall walk, and not faint. Isaiah 40:31

Don't wait in distress, confusion, or doubt. Wait in victory, because you received a Word from the Lord. When you know that you're about to mount up, you won't mind waiting. Even if it takes ten years, wait with praises on your lips. Don't wait around grumbling and complaining, sniffling and crying. No weapon formed against you shall prosper. Wait on God with confidence this morning. Why?

Heaven and earth shall pass away: but my words shall not pass away. Mark 13:31

For I am the LORD: I will speak, and the word that I shall speak shall come to pass; it shall be no more prolonged: for in your days, O rebellious house, will I say the word, and will perform it, saith the Lord GOD. Ezekiel 12:25

Meditate on this next Scripture today:

He also said, "This is what the kingdom of God is like. A man scatters seed on the ground. Night and day, whether he sleeps or gets up, the seed sprouts and grows, though he does not know how. All by itself the soil produces grain—first the stalk, then the head, then the full kernel in the head. As soon as the grain is ripe, he puts the sickle to it, because the harvest has come." Mark 4:26-29 NIV

You may not know how God is working a situation out, but wait on Him nonetheless. You have planted the seed of faith, and it will grow night and day. Wait for its full manifestation—don't pluck it up before its time. Impatience can often abort your seed. Don't allow fear or unbelief to destroy your ground. Make sure that you're not fertilizing your harvest with words of doubt and death, but are constantly watering it with words of faith and life.

Morning Glory

WALKING IN FORGIVENESS

Forgive.

For if ye forgive men their trespasses, your heavenly Father will also forgive you: But if ye forgive not men their trespasses, neither will your Father forgive your trespasses. Matthew 6:14-15

Forgive.

Take heed to yourselves: If thy brother trespass against thee, rebuke him; and if he repent, forgive him. And if he trespass against thee seven times in a day, and seven times in a day turn again to thee, saying, I repent; thou shalt forgive him. Luke 17:3-4

Forgive.

Let all bitterness, and wrath, and anger, and clamour, and evil speaking, be put away from you, with all malice: And be ye kind one to another, tenderhearted, forgiving one another, even as God for Christ's sake hath forgiven you. Ephes. 4:31-32

Let it go. Forgive.

If you're walking around today with unforgiveness in your heart, let it go this morning. God has not forgiven you if you are harboring unforgiveness against someone else. Whether you know it or not, your blessing is connected to other people. Because of the hardness of your heart, not only do you cause unforgiveness to nurture the root of bitterness, wrath, anger, and clamor, but you also are not leadable.

After this manner therefore pray ye: Our Father which art in heaven, Hallowed be thy name. Thy kingdom come. Thy will be done in earth, as it is in heaven. Give us this day our daily bread. And forgive us our debts, as we forgive our debtors. And lead us not into tempta-tion, but deliver us from evil: For thine is the kingdom, and the power, and the glory, for ever. Amen. Matthew 6:9-13

"Lead us not unto temptation." How can the Lord not lead you into temptation when He can't even lead you to forgive-ness? By operating in unforgiveness, you are giving sin the green light to be prevalent in your life. You are out of sequence; you're out of order. Back on up, and forgive. If not, you'll keep falling into things that are not of God, because you don't release Him to lead you not into temptation and deliver you from evil. Whatever it is, let it go. It's not worth you stripping yourself of your hedge of protection. Evil will surely beset you if you do not forgive.

Do you realize that forgiveness is the one command issued in the Lord's prayer? Everything else, God is respon-sible for. However, the one thing that qualifies you to receive anything else in that prayer is your adherence to forgiveness. Don't believe Him for your daily bread, if you can't forgive. How can you be delivered from evil when you're still hung up on the forgiveness clause?

Devotional

I know it may be hard to forgive; some unspeakable things may have been committed against you. The very thought of it may be welling up a gulf of anger and resentment within your heart right now, but, I'm telling you, unforgiveness will kill you. It opens the door to a whole host of evil forces to wreak havoc in your life and torment you. Forgive and allow the Lord to shut that door of your life and open a brand new one in Him.

I know thy works: behold, I have set before thee an open door, and no man can shut it: for thou hast a little strength, and hast kept my word, and hast not denied my name. Rev. 3:8

Your mind may be racing right now with all of the wrongful things people have done to you. The enemy may be telling you that if you forgive them, then they're getting away with it. You may think you're a pushover if you forgive. Arrest those thoughts right now. Forgiveness is beyond our level of understanding, nevertheless, it is required. Come on and lean on the Lord this morning.

Trust in the LORD with all thine heart; and lean not unto thine own understanding. Proverbs 3:5

Yes, you can do it. You can release it. Let it go. Let it go and live this morning. Let it go and be delivered this morning. He'll dry your tears; He'll hearken unto your cry, but you've got to decide to give it to Him. Trust Him, and forgive. Lean on Him, and forgive. Let Him give you the strength to forgive. Give it to Him today. Receive His forgiveness. Do it this morning. Do it for yourself. You are an overcomer; therefore, overcome the stench of the past. Overcome the deeds of the enemy against you. If you do not forgive, you allow the devil to rob you of your soul's salvation. The enemy has already stolen some precious things from you; hasn't he stolen enough?

Please walk in forgiveness. Trust in the Lord. Depend on Him right now. Reach up to His ways this morning. His ways are not our ways, neither are His thoughts our thoughts. Reach up for His strength today. Reach beyond the anger. Reach beyond the despair. Reach beyond your broken heart. Reach up, reach up, reach up. The Lord is there for you. He knows the intimate details of what happened. He's not a god that cannot feel your pain. Give Him that yoke this morning by forgiving. That load is too heavy for you to bear alone. Let Him carry your burden today. Pour out your heart to Him, and He'll pour out His Spirit on you. Cast your cares on Him for He cares for you. Call on Him — He'll answer . . . He's just a prayer away.

If we confess our sins, he is faithful and just to forgive us our sins, and to cleanse us from all unrighteousness. 1 John 1:9

Morning Glory

WALKING IN HUMILITY

*If my people, which are called by my name, shall humble them-
selves, and pray, and seek my face, and turn from their wicked ways;
then will I hear from heaven, and will forgive their sin, and will heal
their land. 2 Chron. 7:14*

Humility is a key component to getting your prayers
answered. The Lord doesn't admonish us to ask Him to make
us humble; He said humble yourself. Humble yourself, then
pray and seek His face. Too many of us are backwards and
out of sync, entering into prayer first without ever having
humbled ourselves. The Lord wants to remind you this
morning that the time has come for you to leave your gift,
calling, and title aside and go before the Lord saying, "It's just
me, Lord. Broken and blemished, here I am."

Pride goeth before destruction, and an haughty spirit before a fall.
Proverbs 16:18

The reason so many of our prayers have been hitting and
missing is because we're not filled with enough humility. God
can't really use some of you because the minute you learn five
Scriptures, you think you're better than everybody else. You
start believing that you don't need to submit, because you
think you're smarter than everyone else anyway. When
you're so puffed up and full of yourself, be careful because
you are setting yourself up for a great, big fall.

We've got to stop coming into God's presence so cockily. You can't have an arrogant, high and mighty, stinking spirit, and think when you get in God's presence, you're able to be a sweet-smelling fragrance before Him. How can you mistreat the brethren, then think you can go before God meek and humble?

But he giveth more grace. Wherefore he saith, God resisteth the proud, but giveth grace unto the humble. James 4:6

For thus saith the high and lofty One that inhabiteth eternity, whose name is Holy; I dwell in the high and holy place, with him also that is of a contrite and humble spirit, to revive the spirit of the humble, and to revive the heart of the contrite ones. Isaiah 57:15

The time has come to end the masquerade. The Lord is not impressed with false humility. Some people don't have a clue what being humble is all about. They think humility is looking frail, fragile, and just plain pitiful, and whispering "God bless you" everywhere they go.

Humility is when you are aware of your own defects. That principle alone rules out self-righteousness, which only focuses on the flaws of others. Self-righteous people aren't apt to help, because they enjoy being better than others. Rather than extending a helping hand to bring someone up, they feel better when they are looking down on people.

When men are cast down, then thou shalt say, There is lifting up; and he shall save the humble person. Job 22:29

Devotional

Humility is lowering your natural state on your own. It's being so rid of pride that you lower your rank and willingly seek to serve.

And whosoever shall exalt himself shall be abased; and he that shall humble himself shall be exalted. Matthew 23:12

Humble yourself today. Humble yourself before the Lord has to humble you; believe me, He certainly knows how. He knows how to take you out of that house and out of that car, and break you all the way down. When you start humbling yourself, you then put yourself in a position where God can trust you. When you possess real humility, you are filled with compassion. You'll look at people struggling, and instead of being their judge and jury, your heart will go out to help them.

Humble yourself today. Remember where God brought you from. Don't be so quick to pass judgement on others and forget all of the mistakes you've made. You are no better than anyone else. It is only by the grace and mercy of the Lord that you are who you are right now.

Can you look at somebody else and say, "I remember when I was struggling like that"? Can you say, "Help that person, Lord. Give him strength, because I remember when I could hardly make it"? Can you remember the times when you used to be up and down and just couldn't get it all together? Humble yourself.

Humble yourselves in the sight of the Lord, and he shall lift you up.
James 4:10

Morning Glory

"WHO DO YOU SAY THAT I AM?"

What do you really want from God? Do you want things, or do you want God? Is He your Santa Claus? Just what is it that you really want? Do you want a well-known name, or do you want a ministry? Are you seeking thrills, or are you seeking God's face?

You may know how to worship and praise the Lord, but as soon as a test hits, do you skip out on God? Can you be found in church, or when you fail, do you abandon it for weeks, then stop showing up altogether? When your back is against the wall, and you have no place to turn, are you still shouting, dancing, and praising the Lord?

When you really know Who God is, you know that whatever situation you're faced with, He's working it out for your good. You don't worry about what's going on, because you know that God shall supply all of your needs.

The Lord has got to be more than just a religion to you. I found out a long time ago that God wasn't in the church name. When I got into a mess, my mother and father couldn't get me out. I had to get down on my face, turn down my plate, and find out Who God was for myself.

You can be in church for years and still not know God. I knew the whole doctrine, but I didn't know the Lord. I knew who the bishop was, but I didn't know God. I knew who the missionary was, but I still didn't know God. Knowing the Lord is a revelation—it's a gift from God. I don't care how much you fast; you can't know Him until He reveals Himself to you. If you've gotten to the place where you know that you know God, you ought to be praising Him every chance you get.

And after eight days again his disciples were within, and Thomas with them: then came Jesus, the doors being shut, and stood in the midst, and said, Peace be unto you. John 20:26

Perhaps you're wondering how you're going to make it because every door seems shut, but guess what? That's when you ought to start thanking the Lord. If the doors are shut, then that means God is getting ready to stand in the midst and speak peace to your situation. While you're busy complaining about not having a way, did you ever stop to consider what Jesus said?

Jesus saith unto him, I am the way, the truth, and the life: no man cometh unto the Father, but by me. John 14:6

When it looks like there is no way, you don't have to ask the Lord to make one—He is the Way. When every door in your life is shut, be reminded that God said:

Devotional

I am the door: by me if any man enter in, he shall be saved, and shall go in and out, and find pasture. John 10:9

The Lord has a question for you this morning:

"But what about you?" he asked. "Who do you say I am?"
                                        Matthew 16:15 NIV

"YES, LORD!"

Go on and tell the Lord "yes" this morning. When you tell Him yes, you're saying no to the devil. When you tell Him yes, the devil can't have the victory. When you tell Him yes, Satan has to take his hands off. When you tell Him yes, the chains of bondage have to drop. When you tell Him yes, your mind is set free. Tell Him yes this morning.

There's deliverance in your "yes, Lord." There's victory in that yes. Overcoming power is in that yes. You may not feel like it, you may not want to say it, but say it to Him anyhow. Say yes. Tell Him yes out of your spirit, and yes out of our soul. I know you may just want to sit there reading this book, but you must participate in your victory this morning. Come on, and tell Him yes.

The Lord is saying, "If you tell Me yes, I'll wipe the tears away. If you tell Me yes, I'll give you victory in the midst of the situation. If you tell Me yes, you'll walk out this morning with unspeakable joy—full of joy and peace."

You may not understand it, but tell Him yes anyway. Some things go beyond your intellect and are picked up by your spirit man. Your yes is what kills the flesh; your "yes, Lord" causes everything that's telling God "no" to die. Your yes is a powerful weapon.

When "yes Lord" comes out of your mouth, that's when

you really start consecrating. That yes goes into every area of your life and says no to fornication, no to lying, no to gossiping, no to being a cheater, no to your flesh, no to falling, no to masturbation, no to getting mad, no to cursing, no to being conniving, no to being deceitful. That yes gets transformed into your spirit man and necessitates your obedience to the Lord.

Your yes tells the Lord that you relinquish your ability to fix whatever situation you're facing. The Lord is saying, "Can I have it?" Yes Lord. "Can I fix it?" Yes Lord. "Can I work this out for you?" Yes Lord. "Will you trust Me with your future?" Yes Lord. "Am I your provider?" Yes Lord. "Am I your deliverer?" Yes Lord. "Well then, My Word says, 'He that hath begun a good work in you shall finish what He has started.' So all I need from you is to tell Me yes."

Understand that the Lord is not some notorious gangster about to run roughshod over your will. He needs your permission. The devil doesn't want you to say yes, because the moment that "yes Lord" comes out of your mouth, he knows that God just killed something. Something in you just died. The devil just lost his hold on you.

Come on and tell Him "Yes, Lord. Yes to Your will, and no to the devil." You may not understand it, but tell Him yes. You may not like it, but tell Him yes. Give it to Him. Defer it to Him. Tell Him yes this morning. Thank Him for that yes going deep into your spirit. Let it penetrate that no out of you. Push it out, shove it out, and pull that yes on in. "Yes, Lord. Yes, Lord. Yes, yes, yes, yes, YES!!!!!!"

Devotional

Morning Glory

Devotional

Other Books by Juanita Bynum

Morning Glory Meditation Scriptures

Morning Glory Prayer Journal

Morning Glory Gift Book

No More Sheets Paperback

No More Sheets Hardback

No More Sheets Devotional

No More Sheets Quote Book

The Juanita Bynum Topical Bible

Don't Get Off the Train

The Planted Seed

My Inheritance

Never Mess with a Man Who Came Out of a Cave

Available at your local bookstore

Author Contact

Morning Glory Ministries
Post Office Box 939
Waycross, GA 31502
912-287-0032